The Reader as DETECTIVE

LEVEL B
Second Edition

Burton Goodman

Former Teacher of English and Coordinator of High School–College Continuum, Bureau of Educational and Vocational Guidance, New York City Public Schools

When ordering this book, please specify:
either **R 608 S** or READER AS DETECTIVE–B

AMSCO SCHOOL PUBLICATIONS, INC.
315 Hudson Street / New York, N.Y. 10013

Illustrations by John Jones

ISBN 1-56765-018-X

New York City Item 56765-018-9

Printed in the United States of America

2 3 4 5 6 7 8 9 10   00 99 98 97 96

TO THE STUDENT

The Reader as Detective has been specially designed to make you a more active reader—to help you become more involved in the reading process.

Today, more than ever, this is important because TV and movies can affect our reading habits. They, and other mass media, sometimes tend to make us passive, less active readers. This is unfortunate because reading is an active, participatory experience. It is not merely viewing or watching.

We believe that a good reader is an *active* reader, and that a good reader is like a good detective.

Think about this. When you read a powerful story of detection, suspense, mystery, or action, you march along with the characters in search of the ending, or solution. You *are*—or *should* become— THE READER AS DETECTIVE. Reading is an adventure—one in which you have become *involved*. Furthermore, the greater your involvement, the better reader you will become—and the more you will enjoy and appreciate reading.

This book will help make *you* THE READER AS DETECTIVE. It does this in a number of ways.

As noted above, the good reader must "march along with the characters in search of the ending, or solution." To encourage you to do this, each story in this volume contains a special and unique feature. It is called "Now it's time for YOU to be The Reader as Detective." This feature appears near the conclusion of each story. It provides you with an opportunity to be a reading detective—to guess how the story will end. After a while, you will learn to look for and discover clues and hints which will help you in this task.

A good reader is like a good detective in another way. To succeed, the detective must be able to gain an overall impression of the case, to recognize clues, identify important details, put events in sequence, draw inferences, and distinguish fact from opinion. Similarly, the effective reader must be a *reading* detective—on the search for the main idea, for supporting details, clues, inferences, and so forth. In a word, the reader, like the detective, must *master the skills* necessary to obtain successful results.

This volume provides ample opportunities for you to master these skills. Following each story are 25 short-answer questions. Questions 1 to 10 (**The Reader as Detective**) offer repeated practice in *the six basic reading skills* essential for achieving reading success. A symbol next to each question identifies the *kind* of reading skill that particular question helps you to develop. Each symbol is related to detection. Here are the symbols and the skills they represent:

THE SHERLOCK HOLMES HAT
    finding the *main idea*

A MAGNIFYING GLASS
    identifying *supporting details*

FINGERPRINTS
    finding *vocabulary clues*

A TRAIL OF FOOTPRINTS
    putting events in *sequence*

ILLUMINATED LIGHTBULB
    drawing *inferences*

SHERLOCK HOLMES PIPE
    distinguishing *fact from opinion*

Questions 11 to 15 (**On the Trail of Story Elements**) help you to track down and understand story elements such as plot, characterization, setting, style, tone, conflict, climax, irony, and theme.

Questions 16 to 25 (**Finding Word Meanings**) help you become a kind of word detective. By using context clues and Cloze (sentence completion and sentence context techniques), you will learn to develop vocabulary skills.

A final section (**Telling About the Case**) offers a wide variety of interesting activities for discussion and writing—projects which will help you review the story.

The current edition contains a number of additional features including new and revised exercises, a Glossary, and easy identification of vocabulary words. To emphasize total communication skills (reading, writing, speaking, and listening), and to encourage cooperative activities, each **Telling About the Case** section has been expanded.

The first story, "The Adventure of the Red-Headed League," introduces the master detective, Sherlock Holmes. To help familiarize you with the format of this volume, the story has been divided into three parts. In each part, you will note the *techniques*, or skills, that Holmes uses to solve the case. You will be encouraged to use similar techniques as you read.

There are 18 stories in this volume, one for every week of the term—or every *other* week of the school year. The stories, and the exercises which follow them, are intended to help you develop an *active, participatory* approach to reading. We are convinced that they can help you develop a very special kind of reading habit—one which will serve you for a lifetime. Now, let's begin. It's time for *you* to become THE READER AS DETECTIVE.

Burton Goodman

ACKNOWLEDGMENTS

Grateful acknowledgment is made to the following sources for permission to reprint copyrighted stories or adaptations of copyrighted stories. Adaptations are by Burton Goodman.

"The President Regrets," page 65. Reprinted by permission of the author, Ellery Queen, and the author's agents, Scott Meredith Literary Agency, Inc., 875 Third Avenue, New York, N.Y. 10022.

"Introducing Ellery's Mom," page 75. Reprinted by permission of the author, Margaret Austin.

Adaptation of "A Retrieved Reformation," page 86. From *Roads of Destiny*, by O. Henry. Reprinted by permission of Doubleday & Company, Inc.

"Phut Phat Concentrates," page 98. Reprinted by permission of the author, Lilian Jackson Braun, and her agent, Blanche C. Gregory, Inc.

"The Disappearing Man," page 111. From "The Disappearing Man" in *The Disappearing Man and Other Mysteries* by Isaac Asimov. Copyright © 1984. Reprinted with permission of Walker and Company.

"Geraldine Moore the Poet," page 120. Reprinted by permission of the author, Toni Cade Bambara.

"A Day's Wait," page 130. Ernest Hemingway, adapted from "A Day's Wait" from *Winner Take Nothing*. Copyright © 1933 Charles Scribner's Sons, renewal copyright © 1961 Mary Hemingway. Reprinted with permission of Charles Scribner's Sons.

"The Tiger's Heart," page 138. Adapted from an article by Jim Kjelgaard in the April 1951 issue of *Esquire*. Copyright © 1951 by Esquire Associates.

"The Town Where No One Got Off," page 150. Reprinted by permission of Don Congdon Associates, Inc. Copyright © 1958 by Ray Bradbury.

"Too Soon a Woman," page 160. Copyright © 1953 by Dorothy M.

Johnson. Copyright © renewed 1981 by Dorothy M. Johnson. Reprinted by permission of McIntosh and Otis, Inc.

"The Wise and the Weak," page 170. By Philip Aponte from *Literary Cavalcade*, 1954. Copyright © 1954 by Scholastic Inc. Reprinted with the permission of the Scholastic Writing Awards Program.

"Louisa, Please Come Home," page 180. From *Come Along with Me* by Shirley Jackson. Copyright © 1960 by Shirley Jackson. Reprinted by permission of Viking Penguin Inc.

"Martinez' Treasure," page 190. By Manuela Williams Crosno from *New Mexico Magazine*, September 1936. All copyrights reserved by the author.

CONTENTS

The Adventure of the Red-Headed League

PART 1

by Arthur Conan Doyle

One day last autumn, I called upon my good friend, Mr. Sherlock Holmes. I found him deep in conversation with a heavyset, elderly gentleman with fiery red hair. I was about to apologize for interrupting them, when Holmes invited me in.

"My dear Watson," he said cordially, "you could not possibly have come at a better time."

"I was afraid that you were busy."

"So I am," he replied. "Very much so."

"Then I will wait in the next room."

"No, not at all." He turned to his visitor. "Mr. Wilson," said Holmes, "Doctor Watson, here, has helped me in many of my most successful cases. I am sure that he will be of the utmost use to me in yours."

The stout gentleman half-rose from his chair and gave me a look of greeting.

"Have a seat on the sofa, Watson," said Holmes, as he settled down into his chair. "I think you will want to hear the story which Mr. Jabez Wilson has been telling me. It is one of the most unusual I have heard in some time. Perhaps, Mr. Wilson, you would be kind enough to begin your story again. I ask, not only because my friend, Doctor Watson, has not heard the opening part, but because the peculiar nature of the story makes me anxious to hear it once more."

Mr. Wilson puffed out his chest with pride, and pulled a wrinkled newspaper page from the inside pocket of his jacket. The page was one which contained a number of advertisements. As Mr. Wilson glanced at them, I took a good look at the man. He seemed to me to be a rather ordinary tradesman. I could find nothing remarkable about Mr. Wilson except his flaming red hair.

Sherlock Holmes smiled as his quick eye took in my inspection. "Mr. Wilson has already informed me that he is a printer," said Holmes. "The faded ink spots on his fingertips revealed as much to me. However, I see that Mr. Wilson was a laborer at one time, that he has been writing a great deal lately, and that he has been to China. Beyond these obvious facts, I can deduce nothing more."

Mr. Wilson was astonished. "How in heaven's name did you know all that, Mr. Holmes?" he asked. "How did you know, for example, that I once was a laborer? For it's true that I worked as a ship's carpenter for years."

"Your hands, my dear sir," replied Holmes. "Your right hand is much larger than your left. You have worked extensively with it, and the muscles are more developed."

"Ah, I see. And how did you know that I had been writing recently?"

"What else can be the meaning of the fact that your right sleeve is so shiny for five inches, while the left sleeve has a worn patch near the elbow where you rest it upon the desk."

"Yes. But how did you know that I had been to China?"

"You have, just above your right wrist, a tattoo of a pink fish. I have studied tattoo marks, and have even written on the subject. That kind of tattoo is done only in China. When, in addition, I see a Chinese coin hanging from your watch chain, the matter becomes even more obvious."

Mr. Wilson laughed heartily. "And I thought that you had done something really clever," he said. "But now I see there is nothing to it."

"Perhaps," said Holmes to me, smiling, "I should not have explained. And now, Mr. Wilson, have you found that advertisement you were seeking?"

"Yes, I have it right here," answered Wilson. His thick finger pointed halfway down the page. "Here it is. This is what started it all. Just read it for yourself."

I took the paper from him and read the following:

TO THE RED-HEADED LEAGUE

Because of the will of the late Ezekiah Hopkins, of Lebanon, Pennsylvania, there is now another opening in the League. It entitles a member to a salary of 10 pounds* a week for fairly easy work. All red-headed men who are sound in body and mind are eligible to apply. Come on Monday at

---

*pounds: English money.

eleven o'clock to the offices of the Red-Headed
League, 7 Fleet Street. Ask for Mr. Duncan Ross.

"What on earth does this mean?" I asked, after I had twice
read over the extraordinary announcement.

Holmes chuckled. "It is a little off the beaten path, isn't
it, Watson," said he. "And now, Mr. Wilson, tell us about
yourself and your household, and the effect that this advertisement has had upon your fortunes."

"It is just as I have been telling you, Mr. Holmes," said
Jabez Wilson, mopping his forehead. "I have a small printing
shop on Coburg Street in London. It's not very large, and for
the past few years business has been poor. I used to have two
assistants, but now I can afford only one. I would have trouble paying him, too, except for the fact that he is willing to
work for half pay to learn the business."

"What is the name of this obliging youth?" asked Sherlock Holmes.

"His name is Vincent Spaulding," replied Wilson. "And
he's not such a youth either. It's hard to say his age, but I can
tell you this. I could not wish for a smarter assistant. I know
very well that he could go elsewhere and earn twice what I
am able to pay him. But if he is satisfied, why should I put
ideas in his head?"

"Why, indeed?" asked Holmes. "You seem most fortunate
in having an assistant who is willing to work for less than the
full market price. That is not a common experience. It seems
to me that your assistant is as unusual as that advertisement
you showed us."

"Oh, he has his faults, too," said Mr. Wilson. "There never
was a fellow so keen on photography. Snapping away with
his camera all the time, and then diving down into the cellar,
like a rabbit into its burrow, to develop the pictures. That's
his main fault. But on the whole, he's a good worker."

"He is still with you, I presume."

"Yes, sir. He and an elderly woman who does a bit of
cooking and keeps the place clean. That's all I have in my
house, for my wife died years ago, and we never had any children. We live very quietly, the three of us, above the shop. We
keep a roof above our heads and try to pay our debts."

"Tell me about this Vincent Spaulding," said Holmes.

"It was Spaulding who first showed me that advertisement. He came into the office just eight weeks ago with this very newspaper in his hand. He says to me:

" 'I wish to the heavens, Mr. Wilson, that *I* was a red-headed man.'

" 'Why is red hair so desirable?' I asked.

" 'Why,' says he, 'there's a vacancy in the Red-Headed League. It's worth quite a bit of money to any man who gets it. If my hair would only change color, there's a nice easy job all ready for me.'

" 'What's it all about?' I asked. You see, Mr. Holmes, I am a very stay-at-home man and didn't know much about what was going on outside.

" 'Have you never heard of the Red-Headed League?' asked Spaulding, his eyes open wide.

" 'Never.'

" 'Why, I'm surprised at that. It's a society open only to men with red hair. Why, you, yourself, could apply for the job.'

" 'And what is it worth?' I asked.

" 'Five hundred pounds a year,' says he. 'Moreover, the work is not very hard. And it need not interfere very much with one's other occupations.'

"Well, as you can imagine, Mr. Holmes, that interested me greatly. Business has not been good for some years, and an extra five hundred pounds would have come in very handy.

" 'Tell me about it,' I said to Spaulding.

" 'Well,' said he, showing me the advertisement, 'you can see for yourself that the League has a vacancy. There is the address where you should apply for details. As far as I can make out, the League was started by an American millionaire named Ezekiah Hopkins. He was very strange in his ways. Hopkins himself was red-headed, and he had a great sympathy for all red-headed men. When he died, it was found that he had left his enormous fortune in the hands of trustees. He gave instructions to provide easy jobs to men whose hair is of that color. From all I hear, it is splendid pay, with very little to do.'

" 'But,' said I, 'there would be thousands of red-headed men who would apply.'

" 'There are not as many as you might think,' he answered. 'You see, it is limited to men born in London. This Hopkins made his fortune in London and he wanted to do the old town a good turn. Besides, I have heard that there is no use applying if your hair is light red, or dark red, or anything but a bright and blazing, fiery red. Now, if you cared to apply, Mr. Wilson, you could just walk in. Wouldn't it be worth your while to put yourself out for the sake of five hundred pounds?'

"Now, gentlemen," said Mr. Wilson, "it is a fact, as you may see for yourselves, that my hair is of a very full and rich tint. Therefore it seemed to me that if there was any competition for the job, I stood as good a chance of getting it as any man I had ever met.

"Vincent Spaulding seemed to know so much about it that I thought he might prove useful. I ordered him to close up the shop for the day, and we started off for the address that was given in the advertisement.

"Well, when we got to Fleet Street, you can imagine my surprise. I never hope to see such a sight as that again, Mr. Holmes. From north, south, east and west, every man who had a shade of red in his hair had tramped to the address to answer the advertisement. Every color of red was there—orange, brick, clay, and so forth. But, as Spaulding had said, there were not many who had a really vivid, flame-colored tint.

"I despaired when I saw how many men were waiting in the street. I would have given up and gone home, but Spaulding would not hear of it. How he did it I could not imagine. But he pushed and pulled and bumped until he got me through the crowd, and right up the steps which led to the office. Upon the stairs we met many men—some going up hopefully, others coming down dejected. We wedged between them as well as we could, and soon we found ourselves in the office."

"Your experience has been a most entertaining one," remarked Sherlock Holmes as Mr. Wilson paused to catch his breath. "Please continue your very interesting story."

"Well," said Jabez Wilson, "there was nothing in the office except a couple of wooden chairs and a table, behind which sat a small, thin man with hair that was even redder than my own. He said a few words to each of the applicants who came in. However, he always seemed to find a reason to disqualify every one. Getting the position did not seem to be so easy after all.

"However, when our turn came, the little man was much more favorable to me than to any of the others. He closed the door as we entered, so that he might have a private word with us.

" 'This is Mr. Jabez Wilson,' said my assistant, 'and he is interested in filling the vacancy in the League.'

" 'And he is admirably suited for it,' the other answered. 'I cannot recall when I have ever seen a head of hair so fine.' He took a step backwards, and gazed at my head until I felt quite ashamed. Suddenly, he came forward and seized my hair with both his hands. He tugged until I yelled with pain.

" 'You must excuse me for taking an obvious precaution,' he said. 'For twice we have been deceived by wigs, and once by dye.' Then the little man shook my hand warmly. 'Congratulations!' he said. 'The job is yours!'

"With that, he stepped over to the window, and shouted at the top of his voice that the vacancy was filled. A groan of disappointment came up from below. Then the men trooped away in all directions. Finally, there was not a red head to be seen except that of the little man and my own.''

Now it's time for *you* to be a reading detective. The following exercises will help you accomplish this. Like Sherlock Holmes, you will learn to look for clues, find details, put events in sequence, and so forth. You will also learn to *anticipate*, or think ahead.

I. The Reader as Detective

Read each question below. Then write the letter of the correct answer to each question. Remember, the symbol next to each question identifies the *kind* of reading skill that particular question helps you to develop. Each symbol is related, or connected, to detection. Let's review the symbols.

 . . . finding the *main idea*

 . . . identifying *supporting details*

 . . . finding *vocabulary clues*

 . . . putting events in *sequence*

 . . . drawing *inferences*

 . . . distinguishing *fact from opinion*

 1. The most striking thing about Jabez Wilson was his
   a. expensive clothing.
   b. gold watch.
   c. bright red hair.

 2. Sherlock Holmes knew that Mr. Wilson had been to China because
   a. Holmes met Wilson there.
   b. Wilson revealed this fact to Holmes.
   c. Holmes saw that Wilson had a tattoo which must have been done there.

3. "You could not possibly have come at a better time," Holmes cordially told Doctor Watson. Which expression best defines the word *cordially?*

   a. in an angry manner
   b. in a friendly manner
   c. in a sad manner

4. Which happened last?

   a. Jabez Wilson and his assistant set out for the office of the League.
   b. Vincent Spaulding showed Mr. Wilson an advertisement in the newspaper.
   c. The little man pulled Mr. Wilson's hair.

5. We may infer that Sherlock Holmes

   a. was a very careful observer.
   b. charged a great deal for his services.
   c. knew Doctor Watson for a very short time.

6. Membership in the Red-Headed League "entitles" a person to a salary of 10 pounds a week. What is the meaning of the word *entitles?*

   a. gives or grants   *c.* borrows or owes
   b. refuses or denies

7. According to Jabez Wilson, Vincent Spaulding was fond of

   a. fishing.   *c.* stamp collecting.
   b. photography.

8. Which of the following statements expresses an opinion?

   a. Doctor Watson and Sherlock Holmes had worked together on a number of cases.
   b. Jabez Wilson was once a ship's carpenter.
   c. Mr. Wilson will probably enjoy his new job with the Red-Headed League.

9. Vincent Spaulding stated that Ezekiah Hopkins

   a. died a poor man.
   b. made a fortune in London.
   c. had no sympathy for red-headed men.

10. This chapter is mainly about

     a. how Sherlock Holmes knew that Jabez Wilson had been writing recently.

     b. how Jabez Wilson learned about the Red-Headed League and how he obtained a job there.

     c. the life and times of Sherlock Holmes.

II. On the Trail of Story Elements

Story elements are the key *ingredients*, or parts, of a story. Examples of story elements are plot, setting, characterization, style, and tone.

Let's look at **plot.** The plot of a story refers to the *main events in the story.* The plot is the chain of incidents upon which the story is based.

Answer the following questions. Each one refers to the plot of "The Adventure of the Red-Headed League." Now you're on the trail of story elements!

11. Which event happened *first* in the plot of the story?

     a. Jabez Wilson pointed to an advertisement on the page.

     b. Doctor Watson called upon Sherlock Holmes.

     c. Holmes asked Jabez Wilson about his assistant.

12. You will discover later that Vincent Spaulding plays a very important part in the plot of the story. Which one of the following is true of Mr. Spaulding? [The correct answer should make you suspicious of Mr. Spaulding.]

     a. He was not a good worker.

     b. He had fiery red hair.

     c. He was willing to work for half pay.

13. When Wilson and Spaulding arrived at Fleet Street, they discovered that

     a. a large crowd had gathered.

     b. nobody was there.

     c. two or three men were waiting.

14. The little man with red hair

    a. gave the job to Mr. Wilson.

    b. refused to speak to any of the candidates who came in.

    c. shouted out the window that the job was still open.

15. Which one of the following facts plays the *most important* part in the plot of the story?

    a. The fact that Mr. Wilson had been to China

    b. The fact that Mr. Wilson had flaming red hair

    c. The fact that Mr. Wilson's left sleeve was worn near the elbow

III. Finding Word Meanings

Now it's time to be a word detective. Below are ten words which appear in Part 1 of "The Adventure of the Red-Headed League." Study the words and the definitions beside them. Then complete the following paragraphs by using each vocabulary word only *once*. The first two words have already been added. They will help you get started. Now you're on your own!

		page
utmost	greatest possible	1
revealed	shown; made known	2
deduce	figure out by reasoning	2
eligible	fit to be chosen	3
desirable	worth having; valuable	5
vacancy	opening	5
competition	effort to obtain something wanted by others	6
dejected	sad	6
applicants	candidates; people who apply for something	7
admirably	excellently	7

Every good mystery story must have a strong *plot*. The tales of Sherlock Holmes are excellently, or __16__ admirably, plotted. This is because Arthur Conan Doyle took the greatest, the __17__ utmost, care in developing his stories. By carefully following the plot line, you, the reader, can figure out, or __18__, the ending.

In "The Adventure of the Red-Headed League," for example, Jabez Wilson applies for a much-sought-after and highly __19__ position in the League. His bright red hair makes Wilson fit to be chosen, or __20__, for the opening. However, many candidates have heard about the job __21__.

At first, Mr. Wilson thinks that his chances are slim and he is disappointed and becomes __22__. However, he obtains the position despite the __23__ from the other __24__. Later, the reason that Mr. Wilson had so little difficulty is __25__. We then realize how carefully the story is plotted.

IV. Telling About the Case

A. A good detective must learn to look for clues. Show that Sherlock Holmes was expert at finding clues and using them to draw conclusions. Give examples.

B. According to Sherlock Holmes, Mr. Wilson's story was one of "the most unusual" he had heard in some time. Discuss what things you found strange or unusual in Mr. Wilson's story.

"A look of grave concern crossed Holmes's face. 'From what you
have told me,' he said, 'I think it very possible that your case is far
more serious than might at first appear.' "

The Adventure of the Red-Headed League

PART 2

"The little man turned toward me. 'My name,' said
he, 'is Mr. Duncan Ross, and I am one of the
trustees of the fund left by Ezekiah Hopkins. When will you
be able to enter upon your new studies, Mr. Wilson?'

" 'Well, that is a little awkward,' said I, 'for I have a business
already.'

" 'Oh, never mind about that!' said Vincent Spaulding. 'I
shall certainly be able to look after that for you.'

" 'What would be the hours?' I asked.

" 'From ten in the morning until two in the afternoon.'

"Now a printer's business is done mostly in the late afternoon, Mr. Holmes; and I knew that my assistant was a good
man who would take care of anything that turned up. So I
said, 'That would suit me very well. What is the pay?'

" 'Ten pounds a week.'

" 'And what is to be done?'

" 'It's rather simple,' said Mr. Ross. 'However, you must
remain in the office, or at least in the building, the entire time.
If you leave, you forfeit the position at once. The will is very
clear upon that point, Mr. Wilson. Do you understand?'

" 'It's only four hours a day, and I should not think of leaving,' said I.

" 'No excuse will avail,' said Mr. Duncan Ross. 'Neither sickness, nor business, nor anything else. There you must stay or you lose your job.'

" 'And the work?'

" 'It is to copy the *Encyclopaedia Britannica*. The first volume is there on that shelf. You must bring your own ink, pens, and paper. But we will provide the table and chair. Will you be ready tomorrow?'

" 'Certainly,' I answered.

" 'Then good-bye, Mr. Jabez Wilson, and let me congratulate you once more on the important position which you have been fortunate enough to gain.' He led me out of the room, and I went home with my assistant, hardly knowing what to say or do, so pleased was I at my own good fortune.

"Well, Mr. Holmes, I thought the matter over all day; and by the evening I was in low spirits. I had come to the conclusion that the whole affair must be some hoax or joke, though what its purpose might be, I could not imagine. It seemed beyond belief that anyone could make such a will, or that someone would pay such a sum of money for doing anything so simple as copying the *Encyclopaedia Britannica*. In the morning, however, I found paper, ink, and pens, and I started off for the office in Fleet Street.

"Well, to my surprise and delight, everything was quite right. The table was set out for me, and Mr. Duncan Ross was there to see me begin. He started me off with the letter *A*. Then he left. But he would drop in from time to time to see that everything was all right. At two o'clock he bade me good-day. He complimented me upon the amount that I had written, and locked the office after me.

"This went on for day after day, Mr. Holmes. And on Saturday, Mr. Ross came in and plunked down ten pounds for my week's work. It was the same the next week, and the same the week after. Every morning I was there at ten, and every afternoon I left at two. After a while, Mr. Ross began to come in only once of a morning. Then, after a time, he did not come in at all. Still, of course, I never dared to leave the room for an instant. For I was never sure when he might come in, and the job was such a good one, I could not risk losing it.

"Eight weeks passed by like this, and I was hoping that I might get along to the *B*'s before very long. I had pretty near filled a whole shelf with my writing. And then, suddenly, the whole business came to an end."

Holmes stared at Mr. Wilson. "To an end?"

"Yes, sir. It was this morning. I went to my work as usual at ten o'clock, but the door was shut and locked. There was a note tacked to the door. Here it is. You can read it for yourself."

He held up a white card with words on it. It said:

THE RED-HEADED LEAGUE IS DISSOLVED

Sherlock Holmes and I looked at the card, and at the unhappy face of Mr. Wilson. Suddenly, the humorous side of the affair so completely overwhelmed us that we burst out into laughter.

"I cannot see that there is anything very funny," cried Mr. Wilson, his face flushing up to the roots of his flaming head. "If you can do nothing better than laugh at me, I can go elsewhere."

"No, no," cried Holmes, easing him back into the chair from which he had half-risen. "I wouldn't miss your case for the world. It is truly refreshing and unusual. But there is, if you will excuse my saying so, something just a little comical about it. What steps did you take when you found the card upon the door?"

"I was staggered, sir. I did not know what to do. I stopped in at all the offices in the building, but no one could tell me anything. Finally, I went to the landlord and asked him if he could tell me what had become of the Red-Headed League. He said he had never heard of any such organization. Then I asked him who Mr. Duncan Ross was. He said that the name was new to him.

" 'Who is the red-headed gentleman whose office is at No. 4?' I inquired.

" 'Oh,' he answered. 'His name is William Martinson. He is a lawyer who had been using that room on a temporary basis until his new office became ready. He moved out yesterday.'

" 'Where could I find him?' I asked.

" 'At his new office. He did tell me the address. Yes—17 King Edward Street.'

"I went there at once, Mr. Holmes. But when I got to that address I found it was a factory and that no one in it had ever heard of either Mr. William Martinson or Mr. Duncan Ross."

"What did you do then?" asked Holmes.

"I went home and discussed the matter with my assistant. But he could not help me in any way. He merely said that if I waited I should probably receive some word by mail. But that was not good enough, Mr. Holmes. I did not wish to lose such a job without a struggle. I had heard that you were good enough to give advice to poor folks who needed it, so I came immediately to you."

"And you acted very wisely," said Holmes. "Your story is an exceedingly interesting one, and I shall be happy to look into it." A look of grave concern crossed Holmes's face. "From what you have told me," he said, "I think it very possible that your case is far more serious than might at first appear."

"It's serious enough!" exclaimed Mr. Jabez Wilson. "Why, I have lost ten pounds a week!"

"As far as you are personally concerned," said Sherlock Holmes, "I do not see that you have any grievance against this extraordinary league. On the contrary, you are, I understand, 80 pounds richer, to say nothing of the knowledge you have gained on every subject which comes under the letter *A*. No, you have lost nothing by them."

"No, sir. But I want to find out about them, who they are, and what their purpose was in playing this joke—if it was, indeed, a joke—upon me. It was for them, you must admit, a pretty expensive prank."

"We shall endeavor to clear up these points for you. But first, one or two questions, Mr. Wilson. This assistant of yours who first called your attention to the advertisement. How long has he been with you?"

"For about three months."

"How did he come?"

"In answer to an advertisement."

"Was he the only applicant?"

"No, I had about a dozen."

"Why did you pick him?"

"Because he was handy and would work cheap."

"At half pay, in fact."

"Yes."

"What is he like, this Vincent Spaulding?"

"He is small, well built, very quick in his ways. His face is always smooth-shaven. He is about thirty, perhaps. He also has a small scar on the right side of his forehead."

Holmes sat up in his chair in considerable excitement. "I thought as much," said he. "Is he still with you?"

"Oh yes, sir. I have only just left him."

"And has your business been attended to in your absence?"

"There's never been anything to complain of, sir."

"That will do, Mr. Wilson. I shall be happy to give you an opinion upon the subject in a day or two. Today is Saturday. I hope that by Monday we may come to a conclusion."

"Well, Watson," said Holmes, after our visitor had left, "what do you make of it?"

"I make nothing of it," I answered frankly. "It's a most mysterious business."

"As a rule," said Holmes, "the more unusual and bizarre a thing is, the less mysterious it eventually proves to be. It is your commonplace crimes which are the most puzzling—just as a commonplace face is the most difficult to identify. But I must act promptly on this matter."

"What are you going to do?" I asked.

"To think," he answered. "Please do not speak to me for fifty minutes."

With that, Holmes curled himself up in his chair, his thin knees drawn up to his hawklike nose. And there he sat with his eyes closed.

I had come to the conclusion that Holmes had fallen asleep. Indeed, I was nodding off myself, when he suddenly sprang out of his chair. He looked like a man who had made up his mind.

"Do you think, Watson," he said, "that your patients could spare you for a few hours?"

"My practice is not very large. I see no one today."

"Then put on your hat. We are going to Coburg Street," said Holmes.

We traveled by subway to Aldergate. From there a short walk took us to Coburg Street, where Jabez Wilson had his shop. It was a short block lined with places of business. At the far corner, a sign with the words "JABEZ WILSON—PRINTING" announced the place where our red-headed visitor carried on his trade.

Sherlock Holmes stopped in front of the shop and looked it all over, his eyes shining brightly. He walked slowly up the street, then down again to the corner, looking keenly at each place. Finally, he returned to Jabez Wilson's establishment. He went up to the door and knocked. It was opened instantly by a clean-shaven young fellow who asked him to step in.

"Thank you," said Holmes. "I wish only, however, to ask directions. Can you tell me how to go from here to the Strand Theatre?"

"Third block on the right, then turn left," the assistant answered promptly, closing the door.

"Smart fellow, that," observed Holmes, as we walked away. "He is, in my judgment, the fourth smartest man in London, and, as for daring, he may well be the third. I have heard something of him before."

"Evidently," said I, "Mr. Wilson's assistant counts for a good deal in the mystery of the Red-Headed League. I am sure that you inquired directions merely that you might see him."

"Not him."

"What then?"

"The knees of his trousers."

"And what did you see?"

"What I expected to see. They were mud-stained and worn. However, my dear Watson," said Holmes, standing on the corner and glancing up the block, "this is a time for observation, not for talk. I should like to remember the exact order of the houses here. It is a hobby of mine to have a precise knowledge of London. Let me see—there is, of course, Mr. Wilson's shop, then the newspaper store, the Coburg branch of the Suburban Bank, then the grocery. And now, you will want to go home, no doubt, Doctor."

"Yes, it would be a good idea."

"And I have some work to do which will take some hours. This business at Coburg Street is serious."

"Why serious, Holmes?"

"I have every reason to believe that a very considerable crime is being contemplated. I believe that we shall be in time to stop it. However, since today is Saturday, that rather complicates matters. I shall need your help tonight."

"At what time?"

"Ten o'clock will be early enough."

"I shall be at your apartment at Baker Street at ten."

"Excellent," said Holmes. He waved his hand and turned on his heel. "And, I say, Doctor," Holmes added, "there may be a little danger tonight. So kindly bring your army revolver."

Then he disappeared among the crowd.

Now it's time for YOU to be The Reader as Detective.

According to Sherlock Holmes, a very serious crime was being planned. Do you have any idea what that crime might be? Here are some clues:

- A *place of business* that Holmes saw on Jabez Wilson's block.
- Vincent Spaulding's knees which were mud-stained and worn.

(Hint: *Why* were Spaulding's knees "mud-stained and worn"? How might this relate to a business establishment on Mr. Wilson's street?)

Try the following exercises. Then read the conclusion to "The Adventure of the Red-Headed League."

I. The Reader as Detective

Read each question below. Then write the letter of the correct answer to each question. Remember, the symbol next to each question identifies the *kind* of reading skill that particular question helps you to develop. Note that each symbol is related, or connected, to detection.

1. How much pay did Jabez Wilson receive?
   a. five pounds a week
   b. ten pounds a week
   c. twenty pounds a week

2. Mr. Wilson was required to work
   a. four hours a day.
   b. eight hours a day.
   c. ten hours a day.

3. Sherlock Holmes believed that "a very serious crime is being contemplated." Which expression best defines the word *contemplated?*
   a. thought about or considered
   b. halted or stopped
   c. asked about or questioned

4. The landlord stated that he
   a. had never heard of the Red-Headed League.
   b. had heard of Mr. Duncan Ross.
   c. was planning to close all the offices in the building.

5. Which sentence expresses an opinion?
   a. Vincent Spaulding had been working for Mr. Wilson for about two months.
   b. Watson stated that he would meet Holmes at ten o'clock.
   c. Someone was probably playing a silly joke on Mr. Wilson.

6. We may infer that Sherlock Holmes

   a. was completely confused about the mystery of the Red-Headed League.

   b. wanted to see what places of business were near Mr. Wilson's shop.

   c. thought that Mr. Wilson's story was boring.

7. Mr. Wilson was afraid that someone was playing a "prank" on him. What is the meaning of the word *prank?*

   a. joke

   b. treat

   c. musical instrument

8. Which happened last?

   a. Mr. Wilson found a white card tacked to the door.

   b. Holmes and Doctor Watson went to Coburg Street.

   c. Duncan Ross congratulated Mr. Wilson on the amount he had written.

9. Most likely, Vincent Spaulding's knees were mud-stained and worn from

   a. printing signs and announcements in the shop.

   b. playing football after work.

   c. digging in the earth.

10. This selection is mainly about

   a. Mr. Wilson's job and what happened after it ended.

   b. how Sherlock Holmes asked Doctor Watson for help.

   c. Mr. Wilson's search for Duncan Ross.

II. On the Trail of Story Elements

You know that plot is one of the key elements in a story.

Another important story element is **characterization.** Characterization refers to the way a character is pictured, or *portrayed.* How a character looks, thinks, and acts go into making up that person's characterization.

Answer the following questions. Each one relates to characterization or plot.

11. Which statement best characterizes Vincent Spaulding?

    a. He was small, smart, smooth-shaven, and around thirty.

    b. He was tall, heavy, and slow moving.

    c. He had a small scar on his forehead and a bright red beard.

12. Which expression characterizes Sherlock Holmes best?

    a. cautious and afraid

    b. unable to reason carefully

    c. thoughtful and clever

13. Jabez Wilson was

    a. very wealthy.

    b. highly intelligent.

    c. not especially bright.

14. Which event happened first in the plot?

    a. Holmes and Watson traveled to Mr. Wilson's shop.

    b. Mr. Wilson found a note which stated that the Red-Headed League was dissolved.

    c. Vincent Spaulding gave Sherlock Holmes directions to the Strand Theatre.

15. At the conclusion of this chapter, Holmes

    a. sat silently in a chair with his eyes closed.

    b. asked Mr. Wilson about his assistant.

    c. asked Watson to bring his army revolver to their meeting.

III. Finding Word Meanings

Now it's time to be a word detective. Listed below are five vocabulary words which appear in Part 2 of "The Adventure of the Red-Headed League" and five *new* vocabulary words for you to learn. Study the words and their definitions. Then complete the following paragraphs by using each vocabulary word only *once*. The first word has already been added.

		page
avail	to make use of	14
temporary	lasting for a short time; not permanent	15
grievance	reason for complaint	16
endeavor	to try hard; make an effort	16
bizarre	very odd or unusual	18
tedious	long and tiring	
supervisor	person in charge	
jubilant	very happy; delighted	
passion	strong liking	
compensation	something given which makes up for something else	

During June, Jacqueline heard about a __16__ temporary summer job at the local library. When she inquired about it, the __17__, Miss Santiago, told her that the job was sometimes boring and __18__. "However," explained Miss Santiago, "you will discover that there is additional __19__ besides the pay. There will be plenty of free time. You can __20__ yourself of it to do some reading."

When she heard that, Jacqueline was more than pleased, she was __21__. The reason Jacqueline was so delighted was that she loved reading. She had a special __22__ for detective stories. She particularly liked cases that were strange and __23__. She would __24__ to find stories like that whenever she could.

"I'll take the job!" declared Jacqueline. It was a wise move. All summer long, she didn't have a single __25__ or complaint.

IV. Telling About the Case

A. Can you think of a reason why someone might pay Mr. Wilson to copy the *Encyclopaedia Britannica*? (Hint: Mr. Wilson was required to *remain in the office* for four hours each day.)

B. Why do you think Sherlock Holmes decided to take a trip to Mr. Wilson's shop?

C. According to Sherlock Holmes, the fact that it was Saturday served to complicate matters. Why do you think this was so?

Later, you may have an opportunity to discuss your answers with your classmates. It will be interesting to see which responses proved correct.

"We were left suddenly in darkness. It was an absolute darkness, a
darkness such as I had never before experienced."

The Adventure of
the Red-Headed
League

PART 3

A s I made my way home, I thought it all over. I
thought about Mr. Jabez Wilson's amazing story of
the Red-Headed League and how he had been copying the *Encyclopaedia Britannica.* I thought about the visit which
Holmes and I had made to Coburg Street and the sinister
words which Holmes had delivered when he parted from me.

I wondered: Where were we going this evening? And to do
what? And why should I go armed? I had heard what Holmes
had heard, and had seen what he had seen. Yet it was clear
that *he* saw not only what had happened, but what was *going*
to happen, while to me the whole business was completely
confused. I knew that Jabez Wilson's assistant played an important part in this puzzle. But how? I tried to reason it out.
Finally, I gave up in despair. I put the matter aside, knowing
that when night came I should receive an explanation.

It was a quarter past nine when I started from home and
made my way to Baker Street, where Holmes lives. When I
arrived, I saw two cabs standing in the street. As I made my
way up the stairs, I found Holmes in conversation with two
men. One I recognized as Walter Jones, a police agent from
Scotland Yard. The other was a tall, thin, sad-faced man. He
wore a shiny hat and an expensive overcoat.

"Ah, our party is complete!" said Holmes. "Watson, I think you know Mr. Jones of Scotland Yard. Let me introduce you to Mr. Merriweather, a director of the Suburban Bank. He is to be our companion in tonight's adventure."

"Our friend, Holmes, here, is a wonderful man for starting a chase," remarked Jones to me.

"I hope it will not prove to be a wild goose chase," observed Merriweather, gloomily.

"You may place considerable confidence in Mr. Holmes, sir," said the police agent. "He has his own methods which are quite extraordinary. I do not exaggerate when I say that, once or twice, he has been more nearly correct than our entire force."

"If you say so, Mr. Jones," replied Mr. Merriweather, not very enthusiastically.

"I think you will find," said Sherlock Holmes, "that tonight's adventure will prove most exciting. Consider it a game, one in which the stakes are quite high. For you, Mr. Merriweather, the stake will be some seventy-five thousand pounds. And for you, Mr. Jones, it will be the man you have been looking for."

"You mean," said Mr. Jones, "John Clay, murderer and thief. He's a remarkable young man. His grandfather was a royal duke, and he himself went to school at Oxford. He's a cunning one, that Mr. Clay. We find signs of him everywhere, though we've never been able to capture the man. I've been on his track for years, and have never set eyes on him yet."

"I hope," said Sherlock Holmes, "that I may provide you with that pleasure tonight. It is past ten, however, and time that we started. If you two will take the first cab, Dr. Watson and I will follow in the second."

Sherlock Holmes was rather quiet during the long drive. He sat back in the cab and hummed some tunes. Finally, he spoke. "This bank director, Merriweather, is personally involved in the matter. I thought it advisable to have Jones with us, too. The fellow is as brave as a bulldog, and he has a grip like a lobster's if he gets his claws on anyone." Holmes peered out through the window. "Here we are now," he said, "and there are Jones and Merriweather already waiting for us."

We had arrived at Coburg Street—the same street which Holmes and I had visited earlier that day. The cabs were dismissed, and, following the lead of Mr. Merriweather, we went down a narrow passage to a side door which he opened for us. Inside, there was a small corridor which led to a massive iron gate. This, Merriweather also opened, and we were led down a flight of winding stone steps which ended at another strong gate.

Mr. Merriweather stopped to light a lantern. He then led us down a dark, earth-smelling passage, and, after opening a third door, into a huge vault or cellar which was filled with heavy boxes and crates.

Holmes held the lantern up high and gazed about him. "You need fear nothing from above, Mr. Merriweather," he observed.

"Nor anything from below," said Mr. Merriweather, knocking his heel against the stones which lined the floor. "Why, dear me," he remarked, looking up in surprise. "It sounds quite hollow!"

"I really must ask you to be a little more quiet!" said Sherlock Holmes sharply. "You have already endangered the success of our operation. I beg you to sit down upon one of these boxes, and not to interfere."

With an injured look upon his face, Mr. Merriweather perched himself upon a crate. At the same time, Holmes fell to his knees upon the floor. With the lantern and a magnifying glass, he began to carefully examine the cracks between the stones.

After a few seconds he seemed satisfied, for he sprang to his feet again.

"We must wait an hour at least," he remarked, "for they can hardly begin until the printer has gone to bed. Then they will not lose a minute. The quicker they do their work, the longer time they will have for their escape.

"We are, Doctor," continued Sherlock Holmes, "as you probably have guessed, in the cellar of the Coburg branch of the Suburban Bank. Mr. Merriweather, as you know, is a director of the bank. He will explain to you that there are very strong reasons why some daring criminals are interested in this cellar at present."

"It is our gold," whispered Mr. Merriweather. "We have received a warning of an attempt to steal the gold."

"Your gold?"

"Yes. We had reason, some months ago, to strengthen our reserves. For that purpose, we borrowed seventy-five thousand gold pieces from the Bank of France. It has become known that we have not yet had occasion to unpack the money, and that it is still lying in our cellar. The crate upon which I sit contains two thousand gold pieces alone. We do not usually keep such a large quantity of gold in any one office. This has been causing us concern."

"And with very good reason," observed Holmes. "And now it is time to make our plans. I expect that within an hour, matters will come to a head. In the meantime, Mr. Merriweather, we must put a screen over the lantern."

"And sit in the dark?"

"I am afraid so. The enemy's preparations have gone so far that we cannot risk the presence of a light. First of all, we must take our positions. These are dangerous men, and though we shall surprise them, they may do us some harm unless we are careful. I shall stand behind this crate, while you conceal yourselves behind those. When I flash a light upon them, close in swiftly. If they fire, Watson, you will have no choice but to use your revolver."

Holmes slipped a screen across the front of the lantern. We were left suddenly in darkness. It was an absolute darkness, a darkness such as I had never before experienced. We waited in the depressing gloom, in the cold, moist air of the vault.

"They have but one way to retreat," whispered Holmes. "That is back through the house and out into Coburg Street. I hope that you have done what I asked you, Jones."

"I have stationed three officers at the front door."

"Then we have prevented any escape," said Holmes. "And now we must be silent and wait."

How long it seemed! It was only an hour and a quarter, but it seemed to me to be half the night. My limbs grew weary and stiff for I was afraid to change my position. I waited in the dark, listening to the breathing of my companions. Suddenly my eyes caught the glint of a light!

At first it was only a bright spot upon the stone pavement. Then it grew longer until it became a yellow line. And then, without any warning, a gash seemed to open between the stones, and a hand appeared in the center of the light. For several moments the hand protruded out of the floor.

There was then a loud, grinding sound, as one of the large, flat stones turned over on its side. It left a square, gaping hole through which streamed the light of a lantern. Over the edge of the hole peeped the smooth-shaven face of the printer's assistant. He looked keenly about, and then, with a hand on either side of the opening, the figure drew itself out. In another instant, he stood at the side of the hole and was pulling up after him a companion, thin and small, with a head of very red hair.

The red-headed man looked around. "It's all clear," he whispered to the other. "Do you have the hammer and the bags?"

At that instant, Holmes suddenly sprang out and grabbed the red-headed intruder by the neck.

"Great Scott!" exclaimed the red-headed man. "Jump! Jump!"

The other dived back down into the hole, and I heard the sound of ripping cloth as Jones grabbed at his shirt. The light flashed upon the barrel of a revolver, but Holmes's stick came down on the man's wrist, and the pistol bounced harmlessly to the floor.

"It's no use, John Clay," said Holmes calmly, "you have no chance at all."

"So I see," the other answered coolly. "But I guess that my pal is all right, though I see you have got a piece of his shirt."

"There are three men waiting for him at the door," said Holmes.

"Oh, indeed. You seem to have thought of everything. I must compliment you."

"And I must compliment you," answered Holmes. "Your red-headed idea was both clever and unique."

"You'll see your pal again in a few moments," said Jones. "Just hold out your hands while I put on these cuffs."

"Don't touch me with your filthy hands," remarked our prisoner, as the handcuffs clattered upon his wrists. "You may not know it, but I have royal blood in my veins. And have the goodness, also, to always say 'sir' and 'please' when you address me."

"All right," said Jones, with a smile on his face. "Would you please march upstairs, *sir*, where we can get a cab to carry your highness to the police station."

"That is better," said John Clay softly. He made a sweeping bow to the three of us, and walked calmly off with Mr. Jones.

Now it's time for YOU to be The Reader as Detective.

How was Sherlock Holmes able to solve "The Adventure of the Red-Headed League?" How did he figure out, or *deduce*, that a bank robbery was being planned and how did he know who planned it? The following clues will help you solve the mystery.

- The fact that Vincent Spaulding was willing to work for half pay
- Spaulding's habit of disappearing into the cellar
- The amazing story of the Red-Headed League—especially the requirement that Mr. Wilson *remain in the office* for four hours each day
- Spaulding's mud-stained and worn trousers
- The sudden closing of the League's office and the disappearance of Duncan Ross
- The fact that the Coburg Bank was on the same block as Mr. Wilson's shop

Did you solve the mystery? Read on to see if you are right!

"You see, Watson," Holmes explained later, as we sat in his apartment in Baker Street, "one thing was perfectly obvious to me from the start. There could be only one reason for that fantastic advertisement from the Red-Headed League, and for the copying of the *Encyclopaedia Britannica*. It *had* to be to get the printer out of his shop for several hours each day. The plan for accomplishing that was no doubt suggested to John Clay by Mr. Wilson's bright red hair. The ten pounds a week they offered him would, they knew, prove too great a lure for him to resist. And what did ten pounds a week mean to them when they figured to gain thousands?"

"So Clay and Spaulding were working together."

"Yes. First they rented the office on Fleet Street. Then they placed the advertisement in the newspaper. Then Spaulding got Wilson to apply for the job. Together they managed to keep Wilson away from the print shop for four hours a day. From the moment I heard that Spaulding was willing to work for half pay, it was obvious to me that he had some very special reason for wanting the job."

"But how could you fathom what their reason was?"

"The man's business was a small one, and there was nothing *in the house* which could account for such elaborate plans at such great expense. It must then be something *out of the house*. What could it be? I thought of the assistant's fondness for photography, and of his trick of vanishing into the cellar. The cellar! That was the cue. He was doing something in the cellar—something which took many hours a day for months on end. What could it be? I could think of nothing except that he was digging a tunnel to some other building.

"I had reasoned that far when we went to visit the printer's shop. I rang the bell, and, as I hoped, the assistant answered it. We had never set eyes on each other before, but I hardly looked at his face. His knees were what I wished to see. You must have noticed how stained with earth and how worn they were. That was the result of hours of digging. The only question was what they were digging for. I walked up the street and saw the Coburg Bank in the middle of the block. I was certain, then, that I had solved the problem. After you left me, I called upon Scotland Yard, and upon the director of the bank, with the results that you have seen."

"But how could you tell that they would make their attempt tonight?" I asked.

"When they closed their League offices, that was the sign that they no longer required Mr. Wilson's presence. In other words, they had completed their tunnel. But it was essential that they use the tunnel soon, as it might be discovered, or the gold might be removed. Saturday would suit them better than any other day, as it would give them two days for their escape. For all these reasons, I expected them to come tonight."

"You figured it out perfectly," I exclaimed. "It is a long chain of reasoning, and yet every link in it is strong."

"As you know, Watson," said Holmes, "my life is one long effort to escape from boredom. These little problems help me to do so."

"And, at the same time, you help people," I said.

Holmes shrugged his shoulders. "We are sometimes successful. Thank you for your assistance, my dear Watson. Thus ends the remarkable adventure of THE RED-HEADED LEAGUE."

I. The Reader as Detective

Read each question below. Then write the letter of the correct answer to each question. Remember, the symbol next to each question identifies the *kind* of reading skill that particular question helps you to develop.

1. Mr. Merriweather was a
   a. police agent.
   b. bank director.
   c. murderer and thief.

2. Doctor Watson and the others waited in the darkness for
   a. an hour and a quarter.
   b. half the night.
   c. the entire day.

3. Which happened last?
   a. Holmes introduced Watson to Walter Jones.
   b. Holmes knocked John Clay's pistol to the ground.
   c. Holmes cautioned Mr. Merriweather to be quiet.

4. At the bank, Mr. Merriweather opened "a massive iron gate." Which expression best defines the word *massive*?

   a. large and heavy
   b. small and weak
   c. old and dirty

5. We may infer that Spaulding and Clay

   a. knew that Holmes would be waiting for them.
   b. had been members of the Red-Headed League for many years.
   c. planned the bank robbery months earlier.

6. Which statement expresses an opinion?

   a. Two cabs were waiting in front of Holmes's apartment.
   b. There were seventy-five thousand gold pieces in the cellar of the bank.
   c. "The Adventure of the Red-Headed League" is the best detective story ever written.

7. For several moments, a hand "protruded out of the floor." What is the meaning of the word *protruded*?

   a. stuck out   *c.* looked
   b. dropped heavily

8. Holmes realized that Mr. Wilson's assistant was

   a. interested in a career as a printer.
   b. practicing to become a photographer.
   c. digging a tunnel.

9. How do you think Spaulding felt when he discovered three police officers waiting for him?

   a. shocked   *b.* relieved   *c.* amused

10. This chapter tells mainly about

   a. the life of John Clay.
   b. why Spaulding was willing to work for half pay.
   c. how Holmes succeeded in capturing two criminals.

II. On the Trail of Story Elements

In addition to plot and characterization, another important story element is **setting.** The setting of a story is *where and when the story takes place.* For example, the setting of a story might be a haunted castle in the year 1500, or the frozen Yukon in the winter of 1908.

Answer the questions below. Questions 11–13 deal with the setting of the story. Questions 14 and 15 refer to plot and characterization.

11. Most of this selection is set in

    a. the cellar of the Coburg branch of the Suburban Bank.

    b. an office on Fleet Street.

    c. a cab on the way from Holmes's apartment.

12. Which group of words best describes the vault into which the group was led?

    a. cold, dark, earth-smelling

    b. bright, well lighted, cheerful

    c. gloomy, poorly lighted, pleasant

13. "The Adventure of the Red-Headed League" is set

    a. at the present time.

    b. about five years ago.

    c. more than 50 years ago.

14. Which of the following is *not* an important event in the plot of the story?

    a. Holmes and his companions quietly waited in the darkness for the robbers.

    b. Holmes grabbed John Clay by the neck and knocked the pistol out of his hand.

    c. Mr. Merriweather was not very confident about Sherlock Holmes's methods.

15. Which statement best characterizes Sherlock Holmes?

    a. He was jealous of Doctor Watson and didn't share his adventures with him.

    b. He was excellent at spotting clues and drawing correct conclusions from them.

    c. He lived a very interesting life, but he found his cases boring.

III. Finding Word Meanings

Now it's time to be a word detective. Below are ten words which appear in Part 3 of "The Adventure of the Red-Headed League." Study the words and the definitions beside them. Then complete the following paragraph by using each word only *once*.

		page
sinister	evil	25
exaggerate	to make something appear greater than it is; go beyond the truth	26
enthusiastically	with great excitement; eagerly	26
advisable	worthy of being listened to	26
endangered	exposed to harm; put into danger	27
depressing	making sad	28
glint	flash of light	28
intruder	a person who forces himself or herself on others without being asked or wanted	29
lure	something that attracts or appeals	31
fathom	to figure out the meaning of	31

Many people read mystery stories eagerly and __16__. This is because mysteries have a very special appeal or __17__. They enable the reader to think along with the detective and to figure out, or __18__ what the ending will be.

Perhaps an especially good time to read a mystery is when the weather is gloomy. A __19__ will come into your eyes when you figure out who the evil, or __20__, criminal is. This will brighten your day.

It may not be __21__, however, to read mysteries when you are alone late at night. At that hour, you may __22__ every squeak. You might suddenly imagine that some outsider or __23__ is near. You might suddenly fear that your life is being threatened or __24__. This can have a very saddening, or __25__, effect on you.

IV. Telling About the Case

Explain how each of the following clues listed on page 30 plays an important part in "The Adventure of the Red-Headed League."

A. The fact that Vincent Spaulding was willing to work for half pay
B. Spaulding's habit of disappearing into the cellar
C. The amazing story of the Red-Headed League—especially the requirement that Mr. Wilson *remain in the office* for four hours each day
D. Spaulding's mud-stained and worn trousers
E. The sudden closing of the League's office and the disappearance of Duncan Ross
F. The fact that the Coburg Bank was on the same block as Mr. Wilson's shop

The Problem of Cell 13

PART 1

by Jacques Futrelle

His name was Professor Augustus S. F. X. Van Dusen, but he was known as "The Thinking Machine." He was a brilliant scientist whose specialty was logic. His motto was: Nothing is impossible! The mind is master of all things!

He first became known for a remarkable exhibition he gave at chess. A newcomer to the game, he had, by the force of irresistible logic, defeated a champion who had devoted a lifetime to its study. The Thinking Machine! That described him well. He spent week after week, month after month, in his modest laboratory. There he produced the ideas that amazed the scientific world.

One evening, two well-known scientists, Dr. Charles Ransome and Mr. Albert Fielding, dropped in to discuss a theory with The Thinking Machine.

"Such a thing is impossible!" declared Dr. Ransome during the course of the conversation.

"Nothing is impossible!" stated The Thinking Machine. "The mind is master of all things."

Dr. Ransome laughed. "I have heard you say such things

before," he said. "But they mean nothing. The mind may be the master of matter, but there are some things which will not yield to any amount of thinking. Some things cannot be *thought* out of existence."

"What, for instance?" demanded The Thinking Machine.

Dr. Ransome was thoughtful for a moment. Finally, he responded. "Well, say prison walls. No man can *think* himself out of a cell. If he could, there would be no prisoners."

"A man can use his brain to leave a cell. That is the same thing."

Dr. Ransome seemed amused.

"Let's suppose a case," he said. "Take a cell where prisoners under sentence of death are confined. Suppose you were locked in such a cell. Could you escape?"

"Certainly," declared The Thinking Machine with conviction.

"Of course," said Mr. Fielding, who entered the conversation for the first time, "you could blow up the cell with explosives. But inside, as a prisoner, you wouldn't have them."

"There would be nothing of that kind. You would treat me precisely as you treat prisoners under sentence of death— and I would escape from the cell."

"Not unless you entered it with tools prepared to get out," said Dr. Ransome.

The Thinking Machine was visibly annoyed; his blue eyes snapped.

"Lock me in any cell in any prison anywhere at any time, and I'll escape in a week," he declared sharply.

Dr. Ransome sat up straight in his chair. "You mean you could actually *think* yourself out?" he asked.

"I would get out," was the response.

"Are you serious?"

"Certainly I am."

Dr. Ransome and Mr. Fielding were silent for a long time.

"Would you be willing to try it?" asked Mr. Fielding, finally.

"Certainly," was the answer.

"Then we will arrange it!" said Dr. Ransome. "You will begin now."

"I'd prefer that it begin tomorrow," said The Thinking Machine, "because . . ."

"No, now!" Mr. Fielding cut in. "You are arrested—without any warning, locked in a cell with no chance to communicate with friends, and left there to experience the identical treatment given to a man under sentence of death. Are you willing?"

"All right, *now*, then," said The Thinking Machine, and he arose.

"Let us say, the death cell in Chisolm Prison."

"The death cell in Chisolm Prison."

"And what will you wear?"

"Just these things," said The Thinking Machine. "Shoes, stockings, trousers, and a shirt."

"You will permit yourself to be searched, of course."

"I am to be treated exactly as all prisoners are treated. No more and no less."

There were some arrangements to be made in the way of obtaining permission for the test. But all three were influential men, and everything was done satisfactorily by telephone. It would be a purely scientific experiment, the prison officials were told. Professor Van Dusen would be the most distinguished prisoner they had ever entertained.

The three men were driven to Chisolm Prison, where the warden was awaiting them. He had been told that the famous Professor Van Dusen was to be his prisoner—if he could keep him—for one week; that the professor had committed no crime, but that he was to be treated exactly as all other prisoners were treated.

"Search him," instructed Dr. Ransome.

The Thinking Machine was carefully searched. Nothing was found in his possession. The pockets of his trousers proved to be empty and the white shirt he was wearing had no pockets. His shoes and stockings were removed, examined, then replaced. As he watched all this, Dr. Ransome almost regretted his part in the affair.

"Are you sure you want to do this?" he asked.

"Absolutely," replied The Thinking Machine.

Dr. Ransome turned to the warden. "In the event he fails and asks for his liberty, you understand you are to set him free."

"I understand," replied the warden.

"I should like," said The Thinking Machine to the warden, "to make three small requests. You may grant them or not, as you wish."

"No special favors, now," warned Mr. Fielding.

"I am asking none," was the stiff response. "I would like to have some tooth powder, and I should like to have one five-dollar bill and two ten-dollar bills."

Dr. Ransome, Mr. Fielding, and the warden exchanged astonished glances. The request for tooth powder was not unusual, but they were surprised at the request for money.

"Is there any man our friend could bribe with twenty-five dollars?"

"Not for twenty-five hundred dollars!" the warden asserted.

"Well, let him have them, then," said Mr. Fielding. "I think they are harmless enough."

"And what is the third request?" asked Dr. Ransome.

"I should like to have my shoes polished."

Again, astonished glances were exchanged. This last request seemed absurd, but they agreed to it. These things having been attended to, The Thinking Machine was led back into the prison from which he had undertaken to escape.

"Here is Cell 13," said the warden, stopping three doors down the steel corridor. "This is where we keep condemned murderers. No one can leave this cell without my permission, and no one in it is permitted to communicate with the outside."

"Will this cell do, gentlemen?" asked The Thinking Machine. There was a touch of sarcasm in his voice.

"Perfectly," was the reply.

The heavy steel door was thrown open. There was a scampering of tiny feet as The Thinking Machine passed into the gloom of the cell. Then the door was closed and double-locked by the warden.

"What is that noise in there?" asked Dr. Ransome, through the bars.

"Rats. Dozens of them," replied The Thinking Machine.

The three men were turning away, when The Thinking Machine called, "What time is it now?"

"Eleven twenty," replied the warden.

"Thank you. I will join you gentlemen in the warden's office at half past eight one week from tonight."

"And if you do not?"

"There is no *if* about it."

Chisolm Prison stood in the center of forty acres of open space. If was four stories tall, and was surrounded by a solid wall of concrete eighteen feet high. On top of the wall was a ten-foot steel fence, topped with barbed wire.

The distance from the prison to the wall was twenty-five feet. This area was used as an exercise ground for prisoners, but it was forbidden to those in Cell 13. At all times of the day there were four armed guards on patrol in the yard, one on each side of the building. By night, the yard was almost as brilliantly lighted as by day. On each of the four walls was a spotlight which illuminated the entire area. The wires which fed the spotlights ran up the sides of the building within metal insulators.

All these things were seen and comprehended by The Thinking Machine as he peered out of his barred window. He gathered, too, that a river lay out there beyond the wall somewhere, because he heard, faintly, the hum of a motorboat, and high up in the air he saw a river bird. From that same direction came the shouts of children at play and the occasional crack of a batted ball. He knew, then, that between the prison wall and the river was an open space of playground.

Chisolm Prison was regarded as absolutely safe. No one had ever escaped from it. The Thinking Machine could readily understand why. The walls of the cell were made of thick concrete, and the bars on the window were of heavy iron.

The Thinking Machine fell to remembering how he had come to the cell. First, there was the wall, with the guard's booth. There were two heavy gates there, both of steel. At these gates there was always one man on guard. The warden's office was in the prison building, and, in order to reach that point, one had to pass another gate of solid steel. From there, to Cell 13, where he was now, one had to pass a heavy wooden door and two steel doors in the halls of the prison. And then there was the double-locked door to Cell 13.

There were then, The Thinking Machine recalled, seven

doors to be overcome before he could pass from Cell 13 into the outer world, a free man. Against this was the fact that he was rarely interrupted. A jailer appeared at his cell door at six in the morning with the prison breakfast. He came again at noon, and again at six. At nine o'clock at night came the inspection tour. That was all.

One by one, these things sank into the brain of The Thinking Machine. He then began a painstaking examination of the cell. There was nothing in it except a solid iron bed. This was so firmly put together, it was impossible to take apart. He studied the roof, the walls, and the floor. Everything was concrete, perfectly solid. After the examination, he sat on the edge of his bed and was lost in thought for a long time.

The Thinking Machine was suddenly disturbed by a rat which ran across his foot and dashed into a dark corner of the cell. After a while, The Thinking Machine squinted steadily into the darkness of the corner where the rat had gone. He was able to make out, in the gloom, many pairs of little beady eyes staring at him.

Then, from his seat on the bed, The Thinking Machine noticed the bottom of his cell door. There was an opening there of two inches between the steel bar and the floor. The Thinking Machine moved swiftly to the corner where he had seen the beady eyes. There was a scampering of tiny feet, the squeals of frightened rodents, and then silence.

None of the rats had gone out of the door. Yet there were none in the cell! There must be, therefore, another way out of the cell, however small. Feeling in the darkness with his long, slender fingers, The Thinking Machine started a search.

At last, he was rewarded. He came upon a small opening in the floor, level with the concrete. It was perfectly round and somewhat larger than a silver dollar. This was the way the rats had gone! He put his finger deep into the opening. It seemed to be an old drainage pipe, dusty and dry.

The Thinking Machine sat on the bed for an hour and thought. Noon came and the jailer appeared. He brought the prison lunch of repulsively plain food.

"Any improvements made here in the last few years?" asked The Thinking Machine when he returned the plate.

"Nothing particularly," replied the jailer. "A new wall was

built about four years ago, and I believe about seven years ago a new system of plumbing was put in."

"Ah!" said the prisoner. "How far is it to the river out there?"

"About three hundred feet. There's a baseball field between the wall and the river."

"The drainage pipes of the prison go to that river, don't they?" asked The Thinking Machine.

"Yes."

"I suppose they are very small."

"Too small to crawl through, if that's what you're thinking," said the jailer, grinning.

"Oh," said The Thinking Machine, as the jailer was leaving, "I get very thirsty here. Would it be possible for you to leave a little water in a bowl for me?"

"I'll ask the warden," replied the jailer.

Half an hour later, he returned. He brought some water in a small earthen bowl.

"The warden says you may keep this bowl, but you must show it to me when I ask for it. If it is broken, you will not receive another."

"Thank you," said The Thinking Machine.

Later that afternoon, an armed guard in the yard looked up at the window and saw the prisoner looking out. He saw a hand raised to the barred window, and noticed something white fluttering to the ground under the window of Cell 13. It proved to be a piece of cloth, evidently a piece of shirt, tied around a five-dollar bill.

With a grim smile, the guard took the cloth and the five-dollar bill to the warden's office. There, together, they deciphered something which was written on the cloth in a funny sort of ink, frequently blurred. It said:

"Finder of this please deliver to Dr. Charles Ransome."

"Ah," said the warden with a chuckle, "this plan of escape has gone wrong." He paused. "But why did he address this to Dr. Ransome?"

"And where did he get the pen and ink to write with?" asked the guard.

The warden studied the writing carefully, then shook his head.

"Well, let's see what he was going to say to Dr. Ransome."
He looked closely at the five-dollar bill. There was some writing across the border of the bill.

"Well, if that—what—what do you think of that?" he asked.

The guard took the bill and read this:

Epa eseot d'net niiy awe htton si sih. T

The warden spent half an hour wondering what kind of code it was. After this, he examined the cloth again. It had been torn from a white shirt—The Thinking Machine's shirt, obviously. But how had the prisoner obtained ink and a pen? He decided to investigate.

The warden went back to Cell 13. There he found The Thinking Machine on his hands and knees, engaged in nothing more interesting than catching rats. The prisoner heard the warden's steps and turned to him quickly. "These rats," he snapped, "are a disgrace. There are scores of them."

"Other men have been able to stand them," said the warden. "Here is another shirt for you—let me have the one you have on."

The prisoner removed the white shirt and put on the striped convict's shirt the warden had brought. The warden eagerly examined The Thinking Machine's shirt and found, to his satisfaction, a torn place in the back.

He then showed the prisoner the five-dollar bill with the strange message on it.

"What did you write this with!" he demanded.

"The guard brought you this, then," said The Thinking Machine.

"He certainly did!" the warden replied, triumphantly. "Now what did you write this with!"

"I should think it your job to find out," replied The Thinking Machine.

The warden struggled to restrain his temper. At last, he managed to compose himself. He then made a thorough search of the prisoner and the cell. He found nothing—not even a match or toothpick which might have been used for a pen. The same mystery surrounded the ink with which the code had been written.

The warden left Cell 13 visibly annoyed. "Anyway," he said softly, "writing notes on a shirt won't get him out, that's certain."

"He's crazy to try to get out of that cell," commented the jailer, who had overheard.

"Of course he can't get out," said the warden. "Still, he's clever. I would like to know what that code says—and what he wrote it with."

Now it's time for YOU to be The Reader as Detective.

Can you figure out how The Thinking Machine obtained "ink?" And what did he use for a pen? Hint—think about the following requests made by Professor Van Dusen:

- to have his shoes polished
- to be given a little water in a bowl

Can you decode the message which was written on the five-dollar bill? Here's a clue to help you break the code:

- If you read *left*, you'll be right. You'll be right to read left.

Try the following exercises. Then read Part 2 of "The Problem of Cell 13."

I. The Reader as Detective

Read each question below. Then write the letter of the correct answer to each question. Remember, the symbol next to each question identifies the *kind* of reading skill that particular question helps you to develop.

1. In all, how many gates separated The Thinking Machine from the outer world?

    a. two gates   *c.* thirteen gates
    b. seven gates

2. The rats got out of the cell by going

    a. between the bars.
    b. under the door.
    c. into the drainage pipe.

3. Although he was extremely angry, the warden "managed to compose himself." As used in this sentence, what is the meaning of the word *compose*?

   a. create music
   b. make calm
   c. place blame

4. Probably, Mr. Fielding insisted that Professor Van Dusen go to Chisolm Prison that very day because

   a. he wanted to punish Professor Van Dusen.
   b. he was going to be busy the next day.
   c. he wanted to make certain that Professor Van Dusen didn't have time to plan an escape.

5. Which happened last?

   a. The warden carefully searched The Thinking Machine's cell.
   b. The jailer brought the prisoner some water in a bowl.
   c. Dr. Charles Ransome and Mr. Albert Fielding visited The Thinking Machine.

6. The Thinking Machine requested

   a. a new shirt.
   b. better food.
   c. that his shoes be polished.

7. Together, the warden and the guard "deciphered" a blurred message which was written on the cloth. Which of the following expressions best defines the word *deciphered*?

   a. threw away
   b. figured out
   c. sold for profit

8. Chisolm Prison was

   a. surrounded by a solid wall of concrete.
   b. in the center of 40 acres of open space.
   c. both of the above.

9. Which one of the following quotations does *not* express an opinion?

    a. "The mind is master of all things," stated The Thinking Machine.

    b. "Of course he can't get out," said the warden.

    c. "There's a baseball field between the wall and the river," said the jailer.

10. Suppose this selection appeared as a news article in a newspaper. Which of the following would make the best headline?

    a. Warden Attempts To Figure Out Prisoner's Message Without Success

    b. Dr. Ransome Disagrees with Professor Van Dusen

    c. Professor Van Dusen Plans Prison Escape as Experiment

II. On the Trail of Story Elements

Answer the following questions. They will help you review **characterization** in a story.

11. Which statement best characterizes the professor?

    a. Although he was very smart, he did not have much confidence in himself.

    b. He believed that by using his brain he could accomplish anything.

    c. He had a great deal of money and lived in a large house.

12. The Thinking Machine is best described as

    a. a hardened criminal.   *c.* a professor of English.

    b. a famous scientist.

13. Which group of words best characterizes Professor Van Dusen?

    a. intelligent, lazy, easily discouraged

    b. friendly, silly, thoughtless

    c. brilliant, hard working, remarkable

14. Dr. Ransome and Mr. Fielding

    a. always agreed with The Thinking Machine.

    b. hated The Thinking Machine and played a cruel trick on him.

    c. challenged Professor Van Dusen to prove his theory.

15. Which of the following was true of the warden?

    a. He thought it likely that The Thinking Machine would escape.

    b. He was certain that The Thinking Machine would escape.

    c. He did not think it possible for The Thinking Machine to escape.

III. Finding Word Meanings

Now it's time to be a word detective. Below are ten words which appear in Part 1 of "The Problem of Cell 13." Study the words and the definitions beside them. Then complete the following paragraphs by using each word only *once*.

		page
logic	correct reasoning	37
irresistible	too strong to be held back; very powerful	37
conviction	firm belief	38
precisely	exactly	38
response	answer	38
identical	the very same	39
distinguished	famous or important; well known	39
asserted	stated strongly; declared firmly	40
absurd	foolish; ridiculous	40
restrain	to hold back	45

Do you have a very strong, or __16__, desire to be a famous and __17__ scientist? If your __18__ was "Yes" then you should meet my friend, Freddy. That's __19__ what he wants to be!

Ever since he was very young, Freddy has repeatedly stated and __20__ that he will be a success. He always bubbles over with confidence and __21__ . When he talks about his future, he can hardly hold back, or __22__ himself.

Freddy sometimes does things that are silly or __23__ . He is not known for his clear thinking or __24__ . Still, I'm sure he'll make it some day. Then everyone will say the very same, or __25__ , thing: Freddy F. Farmer is famous—but fun.

IV. Telling About the Case

A. Professor Van Dusen believed that nothing is impossible to the power of the mind. What did he mean by this? Explain why you agree or disagree with him.

B. The main character in this selection is known as "The Thinking Machine." Give examples, drawn from the story, to show that this name was appropriate. It may be helpful to make a list of the items you wish to include.

" 'Watch this!' he said. He kicked in the steel bars in the bottom of the cell door. He swept his hand across the cell window and every bar came out."

The Problem of Cell 13

PART 2

On the fifth day that he had been confined in prison, The Thinking Machine called through the window of his cell to the guard outside.

"What day of the month is it?" he inquired.

"The fifteenth," said the guard.

The Thinking Machine made a mental calculation and satisfied himself that the moon would not rise until after nine o'clock that night. Then he asked another question.

"Who takes care of those lights on the wall?"

"A man from the electric company."

"You have no electricians of your own in the prison?"

"No."

"It seems to me you could save money if you had your own service person."

"That's none of my business," the guard replied.

The guard noticed The Thinking Machine at the window frequently that day. The face seemed tired, and there was a certain wistfulness in the eyes. The guard had seen that look in the face of other prisoners; it was the longing for the outside world.

On the sixth day, the warden received a telephone message. It stated that Dr. Charles Ransome and Mr. Albert Fielding would arrive at Chisolm Prison the following evening. In the event that Professor Van Dusen had not yet escaped—and they presumed he had not, for they had not heard from him—they would meet him there.

"In the event he had not yet escaped." The warden smiled grimly. "Escaped! Ha!"

On the afternoon of the seventh day, the warden passed Cell 13 and glanced in. The Thinking Machine was lying on the iron bed, apparently sleeping lightly. A ray of light came through the cell window and fell on the face of the sleeping man. It occurred to the warden for the first time that his prisoner appeared haggard and weary. There was no way he would get out of that cell by half-past eight!

That evening, at six o'clock, the warden saw the jailer.

"Everything all right in Cell 13?" asked the warden.

"Yes, sir," replied the jailer. "The prisoner didn't eat much, though."

It was with a feeling of relief that the warden greeted Dr. Ransome and Mr. Fielding shortly after seven o'clock. He was about to tell them the full story of what had happened, when the guard from the river side of the yard entered the office.

"The spotlight on my side of the yard doesn't work," he informed the warden.

"Blast it! That man's a jinx!" thundered the warden.

The warden phoned the electric company.

"This is Chisolm Prison," he said. "Send three or four men here to fix a spotlight—and do it quickly!"

Dr. Ransome and Mr. Fielding waited in the office, while the warden went out into the yard. When the warden returned, it was nearly eight o'clock. The electricians had arrived and were now at work. The warden picked up the phone and dialed the guard at the outer booth.

"How many electricians came in?" he asked. "Four? In overalls and wearing heavy boots? All right. Be certain that only four go out. That's all."

He turned to Dr. Ransome and Mr. Fielding. "We have to be careful here—particularly," and there was broad sarcasm in his voice, "since we have a scientist locked up."

The warden stepped out into the corridor. "Run down to Cell 13 and see if that man's in there!" he called sharply to the guard.

Just then a buzz on the telephone from the outer gate

sounded. The warden picked up the receiver.

"Hello! Two reporters, eh? Let them come in. What's that you say?" He suddenly turned pale and looked at the doctor and Mr. Fielding. "The man *can't* be out! He must be in his cell!"

At that moment, the guard returned.

"The prisoner's still in his cell, sir. I saw him. He's lying down."

"There, I told you so!" said the warden, and he breathed freely again.

A moment later, there was a rap on the steel door which led from the jail yard into the warden's office.

"It's the reporters," said the warden. "Let them in."

The door opened and two men entered.

"Good evening, gentlemen," said one. That was the news-paperman, Hutchinson Hatch. The warden knew him well.

"Hello," said the other. "I'm here."

It was The Thinking Machine!

The warden sat with his mouth wide open. Dr. Ransome and Mr. Fielding were amazed; the warden seemed paralyzed. Hutchinson Hatch, the reporter, took in the scene with greedy eyes.

"How—how did you do it?" gasped the warden, finally.

"Come with me back to the cell," said The Thinking Machine.

The warden, in a trance, led the way.

"Now flash your light in there," directed The Thinking Machine.

The warden did so and there—there on the bed—lay the figure of The Thinking Machine There was his bright blond hair.

The warden, with trembling hands, unlocked the cell. The Thinking Machine went inside.

"Watch this!" he said.

He kicked in the steel bars in the bottom of the cell door. "And this too," said The Thinking Machine, as he stood on the bed to reach the small window. He swept his hand across the opening and every bar came out.

"What's this in the bed?" demanded the warden, who was slowly recovering.

"A wig," was the reply. "Turn down the cover."

The warden did so. Beneath it lay a large coil of strong rope, three files, ten feet of electric wire, a thin pair of steel pliers, and a small hammer.

"How did you do it?" demanded the warden.

"Don't think you can hold any man who can use his brain," said The Thinking Machine. "Let's go back to your office. We shall be more comfortable there."

It was an impatient group which stared at The Thinking Machine.

"Do you admit it was a fair test?" he asked.

"I do," said Dr. Ransome.

"Suppose you tell us how—" began Mr. Fielding.

"Yes, tell us how," said the warden.

"Tell us, indeed," said Hutchinson Hatch.

The Thinking Machine took a deep breath, then began.

Now it's time for YOU to be The Reader as Detective.

How did The Thinking Machine escape from the death cell at Chisolm Prison?

The following clues will help you solve "The Problem of Cell 13":

1. The Thinking Machine's request that his shoes be polished
2. His request for some water in a bowl
3. The rats in the cell
4. The drainpipe
5. The playground nearby
6. The feed wire to the spotlight

Each of these clues played an important part in The Thinking Machine's plan. Each helped him escape.

Now read the conclusion to "The Problem of Cell 13."

"When I went into the cell, I asked for tooth powder, two ten- and one five-dollar bills, and to have my shoes polished. Even if these requests had been refused, it would not have mattered seriously. But you agreed to them.

"I knew there was nothing in the cell which you thought I might use. So when the warden locked the cell door on me, I was apparently helpless.

"I was awakened the next morning at six o'clock by the jailer with my breakfast. He told me that lunch was at twelve and dinner at six. Between these times, I gathered, I would be pretty much to myself. So immediately after breakfast, I examined my surroundings from my cell window. One look told me it would be useless to try to scale the wall, for my purpose was to leave not only the cell, but the prison. Of course, I could have gone over the wall, but it would have taken me longer to make my plans that way. I therefore dismissed that idea.

"From this first observation I learned that there was a river on this side of the prison and there was also a playground there. This was later verified by the jailer. But the outside thing which most attracted my attention was the feed wire to the spotlight. It ran two or three feet from my cell window. I knew that would be valuable—in the event I found it necessary to cut off the spotlight."

"You shut it off tonight, then?" asked the warden.

The Thinking Machine ignored the interruption. "While I was thinking about these things, a rat ran across my foot. It suggested a line of thought. There were at least half a dozen rats in the cell—I could see their beady eyes. I frightened them purposely and watched the cell door to see if they went out that way. They did not, but they were gone. Obviously they went another way. Another way meant another opening.

"I searched for this opening and found it. It was an old drainpipe, long unused and partly clogged with dirt and dust. But this was the way the rats had come. They came from somewhere. Where? This one probably led to the river, or near it. The rats must therefore have come from that direction.

"When the jailer came with my lunch he told me two important things, although he didn't know it. One was that a new system of plumbing had been put in the prison seven years ago. The other was that the river was only three hundred feet away. I was positive then that the pipe was part of an old system and that it slanted toward the river. But did the pipe end in the water or on land?"

"How did you discover the answer?" asked Mr. Fielding.

"Easily," replied The Thinking Machine. "I caught several rats in the cell and examined them. They were perfectly dry. Most important, they were *field* rats. The other end of the pipe, then, was on land, outside the prison walls. So far, so good.

"To be able to work freely from this point on, it was necessary to direct the warden's attention in another direction. The first thing was to try to make him think that I was trying to communicate with you, Dr. Ransome. Therefore, I wrote a note on a piece of cloth which I tore from my shirt. I addressed it to Dr. Ransome. Then I tied it around a five-dollar bill and threw it out the window. I knew the guard would take it to the warden. Have you that note, warden?"

The warden produced the note with the strange message.

Epa eseot d'net niiy awe htton si sih. T

"What in the world does it mean anyhow?" he asked.

"Read it backwards beginning with the 'T' in the signature, and disregard the division into words."

The warden did so.

"T-h-i-s—this," he spelled. "This-is-not-the-way-I-intend-to-escape."

"Well, what do you think of that!" said the warden, grinning.

"What did you write it with?" asked Dr. Ransome.

"This," said the former prisoner, and he extended his foot. On it was the shoe he had worn in prison, though the polish was gone—scraped clean. "The black shoe polish, mixed with a little water—thank you for the water—was my ink. The tip of the shoelace made a fairly good pen."

The warden looked up and suddenly burst into a laugh. "You're a wonder," he said, admiringly. "Go on."

"That led you to search my cell as I had intended. I was eager for such a search for I knew that, finding nothing, you would become disgusted and would not try again."

The warden looked at the men with a sheepish grin.

"He then took my white shirt away and gave me a prison shirt. But while he was searching my cell, I had a piece of the lining from that shirt, rolled up into a small ball in my mouth."

"A piece of lining from that shirt!" exclaimed the warden. "Who would have thought it!"

"I then took my first serious step toward freedom," said Professor Van Dusen. "I knew, within reason, that the drainpipe led somewhere near the playground outside. I knew a great many children played there. I knew that rats came into my cell from out there. Could I communicate with someone outside?

"The first thing I needed was thread, so . . ." He pulled up his trouser legs and we saw, at once, that the tops of both stockings, of fine, strong cotton, were gone. "I unraveled them," said Professor Van Dusen, smiling. "After I got them started it wasn't difficult, and I soon had a quarter of a mile of thread that I could depend upon.

"Then, on the piece of lining I had hidden in my mouth, I wrote, with great difficulty, I assure you, a letter explaining my situation to this gentleman here." The Thinking Machine pointed to Hutchinson Hatch. "I knew he would assist me, for it would make an excellent story. I tied the cloth around a ten-dollar bill—there is no surer way of attracting the eye of anyone—and wrote on the cloth: 'Finder of this deliver to the reporter, Hutchinson Hatch, at the *Daily American*. He will give you another ten dollars for the information.'

"The next thing was to get this note outside to that playground where a child might find it. There were two ways, but I chose the better. I took one of the rats—I became adept at catching them—tied the cloth and money to one leg, fastened my thread to another, and turned him loose in the drainpipe. I reasoned that the natural fright of the rodent would make him run until he was outside the pipe. Once outside, he would probably stop to gnaw off the cloth.

"From the moment the rat disappeared into that dusty pipe, I became anxious. There were so many obstacles. The rat might gnaw the string, of which I held one end. The rat might run out of the pipe and leave the cloth and money where

they would never be found. A thousand other things might happen. So began some nervous hours. I had carefully instructed Mr. Hatch what to do if the note reached him. The question was: Would it reach him?

"This done, I could only wait and make other plans in case this one failed. When I went to bed that night I couldn't sleep, waiting for that slight tug on the thread which would tell me that Mr. Hatch had received the note. It was half-past three, I judge, when I eventually felt that tug. And no prisoner under actual sentence of death ever welcomed a thing more heartily."

The Thinking Machine stopped and turned to the reporter.

"You'd better explain what you did, Mr. Hatch," he said.

"The cloth note was brought to me by a small boy who had been playing baseball," said Mr. Hatch. "I immediately saw a story in it, so I gave the boy another ten dollars. I then got several spools of silk, some cord, and a roll of thin, strong wire. The professor's note suggested that I have the finder of the note show me exactly where it was picked up, and told me to begin my search there at two o'clock in the morning. If I found the other end of the thread, I was to pull it very gently two times.

"I began to search with a small flashlight. It was an hour and twenty minutes before I found the end of the drainpipe, half-hidden in the weeds. The pipe was very large there, about ten inches across. Then I found the end of the thread, tugged it as directed, and immediately got an answering pull.

"I then tied the silk to the thread, and Professor Van Dusen began to pull it into his cell. I nearly died for fear that the string would break. To the end of the silk I fastened the cord, and when that had been pulled in I tied on the wire. When that was drawn into the pipe, we had a strong line which ran from the mouth of the drain into the cell."

The Thinking Machine raised his hand and Hatch stopped.

"Having established this line, it is easy to see how I got things into the cell. Cutting the steel bars on the window and door was fairly easy with nitric acid, which I got through the pipe in thin bottles. I used the tooth powder to prevent the acid from spreading. I noticed that the jailer always tried the door by shaking the upper part of the bars, never the lower ones. Therefore, I cut the lower bars, leaving them hanging in place by thin strips of metal.

"I cut the feed wire to the spotlight with acid, too. I did it when the current was off. Therefore when the current was turned on, the spotlight didn't work. I knew it would take some time to find out what the matter was and to make the repairs. When the guard went to report to you, the yard was dark. I crept out through the window—it was a tight fit, too—replaced the bars while standing on the narrow ledge, then waited in the shadows until the electricians arrived. Mr. Hatch was one of them.

"When I saw him I called out, and he handed me a cap and overalls. These I put on within ten feet of you, warden. Together, posing as workmen, we went out the gate to get something from the wagon. The guard let us through without question. We changed our clothing and asked to see you. The wig, and those other things in my bed, I drew up through the pipe, of course."

There was silence for several minutes. Dr. Ransome was the first to speak.

"Wonderful!" he exclaimed. "Perfectly amazing."

"How was Mr. Hatch able to come in with the electricians?" asked Mr. Fielding.

"His newspaper arranged it," said The Thinking Machine.

"But what if there had been no Mr. Hatch on the outside to help?"

"Every prisoner has one friend on the outside who would help him escape."

"Suppose—just suppose—there had been no old plumbing system there," said the warden. "Then what?"

The Thinking Machine seemed amused. "There were two *other* ways out!" he said, smiling.

I. The Reader as Detective

Read each question below. Then write the letter of the correct answer to each question. Remember, the symbol next to each question identifies the *kind* of reading skill that particular question helps you to develop.

1. This selection is mainly about how Professor Van Dusen

    a. thought of a plan, and how he carried it out.

    b. used the tops of his stockings to supply a quarter mile of thread.

    c. wrote a note to the reporter, Hutchinson Hatch.

2. What did The Thinking Machine use for a pen?

    a. a toothpick

    b. a thin piece of metal

    c. the tip of a shoelace

3. Which one of the following did *not* play an important part in the professor's plan?

    a. a wig   *b.* a notebook   *c.* nitric acid

4. The warden thought that the prisoner looked "haggard and weary." Which expression best defines the word *haggard?*

    a. pleased and delighted

    b. tired and worn out

    c. lively and fresh

5. After Hutchinson Hatch located the drainpipe, he

    a. found the end of the thread.

    b. went straight to the prison.

    c. gave a small boy ten dollars.

6. It is fair to say that, in this story, a rat served as a

    a. pet.   *b.* messenger.   *c.* convict.

7. The prisoner's eyes seemed to have "a certain wistfulness"—a longing for the outside world. What is the meaning of the word *wistfulness?*

    a. desire   *b.* hatred   *c.* doubt

8. Which one of the following statements expresses a fact rather than an opinion?

    a. It is much easier to escape from prison than most people think.

    b. There would be far fewer crimes if there were harsher prison sentences.

    c. At Chisolm Prison, breakfast is served at six o'clock in the morning.

9. To figure out the message which was written on the five-dollar bill, it is necessary to

    a. know a special code.

    b. be familiar with a foreign language.

    c. read the message backwards.

10. The last paragraph of the story suggests that The Thinking Machine

    a. could have escaped from Chisolm Prison in several ways.

    b. knew that there was just one way to get out of Chisolm Prison.

    c. did not have confidence that his plan would work.

II. On The Trail of Story Elements

At this point, you have learned to recognize three story elements: plot, characterization, and setting. The following questions serve as a review.

11. What is the setting of this selection?

    a. Professor Van Dusen's laboratory

    b. Chisolm Prison

    c. the office of Hutchinson Hatch

12. Who is the main, or most important, character in the story?

    a. Mr. Fielding

    b. the warden

    c. The Thinking Machine

13. During the course of a story, a character sometimes *changes.* Which statement correctly describes how Dr. Ransome changed?

  a. He was friendly with The Thinking Machine at first; he later grew to dislike him.

  b. He first doubted The Thinking Machine's ability; he later admired it.

  c. He first agreed with The Thinking Machine; he later argued with him.

14. Which one of the following facts plays the *most important* part in the plot of the story?

  a. the fact that an old, unused drainpipe led outside the prison

  b. the fact that the warden couldn't figure out the message tied to the five-dollar bill

  c. the fact that The Thinking Machine had blond hair

15. Which of the following is *not* a key event in the plot of the story?

  a. The Thinking Machine cut the wire to the spotlight.

  b. Hutchinson Hatch tugged the end of the thread.

  c. The warden asked the jailer if everything was all right.

III. Finding Word Meanings

Now it's time to be a word detective. Listed below are five vocabulary words which appear in "The Problem of Cell 13," Part 2, and five *new* vocabulary words for you to learn. Study the words and their definitions. Then complete the following paragraphs by using each vocabulary word only *once.*

		page
confined	shut in	51
verified	proved to be true	55
adept	highly skilled; expert	57
obstacles	things that stand in the way or hinder	57
eventually	finally; at the end	59
liberate	to set free	

infinite	endless; vast
analyzed	examined very carefully
overcome	to conquer
devised	planned

The Thinking Machine was very expert, or __16__, at handling difficult situations. He believed that the mind had vast, or __17__, power. He believed that it could master, or __18__, any problems or __19__.

To prove his theory, The Thinking Machine agreed to be locked up at Chisolm Prison. Although he was __20__ to a concrete cell, he was confident that he would be able to __21__ himself.

First, The Thinking Machine carefully examined, or __22__ his situation. Then he planned, or __23__, an escape. It all worked out __24__. Thus, by the end of the story, The Thinking Machine proved, or __25__ his theory.

IV. Telling About the Case

A. At the beginning of this selection, The Thinking Machine "satisfied himself that the moon would not rise until nine o'clock that night." Explain why this information was important—and pleasing—to The Thinking Machine.

B. Carefully describe how The Thinking Machine escaped from Chisolm Prison. In your answer, show how each of the following clues played an important part in his plan.

1. The Thinking Machine's request that his shoes be polished
2. his request for some water in a bowl
3. the rats in the cell
4. the drainpipe
5. the playground nearby
6. the feed wire to the spotlight

The President Regrets

by Ellery Queen

The Puzzle Club is a group of very important people.
They are drawn together by one passion—to mystify
one another. Their pleasure, in short, is puzzles.

Application to the Club is by invitation only, and membership must be won. The applicant must submit to the Ordeal by Puzzle. If he passes the test, it earns him admission.

Shortly after Ellery Queen became the Puzzle Club's sixth
member, it was decided to invite the President of the United
States to apply for membership.

This was not done lightly. The members took their puzzles
seriously, and the President was known to love mysteries of
all kinds. Besides, the founder of the Club, millionaire oil man
Syres, had been friendly with the President since their boyhood days.

The invitation was sent to Washington. Rather to Ellery's
surprise, the President promptly accepted the challenge. But
later, when Ellery arrived at Syres's Park Avenue penthouse
where the other members had gathered, he was greeted with
gloomy news. The President regretted that he could not make
it that evening after all. A Secret Service man had brought
the message that a problem in the Middle East had suddenly
come up. It had caused the President to cancel his flight to
New York.

65

"What shall we do now?" asked Darnell, the famous criminal lawyer.

"It's too bad that Dr. Arkavy is still at that conference in Moscow," said Emmy Wandermere, the poet. "Dr. Arkavy has such a fine mind, he could always come up with something on the spur of the moment."

"Maybe our newest member can help us out," said their host, Syres. "What do you say, Queen? From your long experience as a writer and a detective, you must have a hundred puzzles at your fingertips."

"Let me think." Ellery considered. Then he chuckled. "All right. Give me a few minutes to work out the details. . ." It took him far less. "I'm ready. I suggest we work together to begin with. Since this is going to be a murder mystery, we will obviously require a victim. Any suggestions?"

"A woman, of course," the lady poet said at once.

"A very glamorous one," said Dr. Vreeland, the well-known psychiatrist.

"That," said the criminal lawyer, "would seem to call for a Hollywood movie star."

"Good enough," Ellery said. "And a glamorous star of the

screen calls for a glamorous name. Let's call her . . . oh, Valetta Van Buren. Agreed?''

"Valetta Van Buren." Miss Wandermere considered. "Yes.
Perfect.''

"Well," Ellery went on, "Valetta is in New York to attend
the opening of her latest picture. She also plans to appear on
TV to promote it. But this hasn't proved an ordinary publicity
tour. In fact, Valetta has had a frightening experience. It so
shook her up that she wrote me a letter about it. I received it
just this morning.''

"What did she say?" asked Dr. Vreeland.

"That during her visit to New York, she was escorted
about town by four men—"

"Who are all, naturally, in love with her?" asked the lady
poet.

"You guessed it, Miss Wandermere. She identified the four
in her letter. One is the playboy, John Thrushbottom Taylor
the Third. And if you haven't heard of Mr. Taylor, it's because
I just made him up. The second is the fabulous Wall Street
success named . . . well, let's call him A. Palmer Harrison. The
third, of course, is the popular artist, Leonardo Price. And the
last of the quartet is—let's see—Biff Wilson, the professional
football player.''

"A likely story," grinned oil man Syres.

"Now," Ellery said, "having named the four men for me,
Valetta went on to say that yesterday all four proposed marriage to her. Unhappily, Valetta was not serious about any of
them. She rejected all four. It was a busy day for Miss Van
Buren. She would have enjoyed it except for one thing.''

"One of them," said the criminal lawyer, "turned ugly.''

"Exactly, Darnell. Valetta wrote me that three of them
took their turndowns gracefully. But the fourth flew into a
rage and threatened to kill her. She was terrified that he
would try to carry out his threat. She asked me to get in touch
with her at once. She hesitated to go to the police because of
the bad publicity it would bring her.''

"What happened then?" asked Syres.

"I phoned her, of course," Ellery replied. "As soon as I
finished reading her letter. Would you believe it? I was too
late. She was murdered last night, a short time after she
mailed the letter.''

"How," asked Darnell, "was the foul deed done?"

"The weapon is unimportant," said Queen. "However, I will say this: Valetta was murdered by the admirer who threatened her life."

"And is that all?" asked the oil man.

"No. I've saved the most important part for last, Mr. Syres. Valetta's letter gave me one clue. In writing about the four men, she said she'd noticed that *she had something in common with three of the four*—and that the fourth was the one who had threatened her."

"Oh," said Dr. Vreeland. "Then all we have to do is find out what they had in common. The three sharing it with Valetta would be innocent. The one left over would have to be the guilty man."

Ellery nodded. "And now—any questions?"

"I take it," the lady poet said, "that we may disregard the possibility that Valetta and three of the men were of the same age. Or had the same hair color. Or came from the same town or state. That sort of thing."

Ellery laughed. "Yes. You may disregard those."

"What about social position?" the millionaire ventured. "Three of the men you described—Playboy John Something Taylor, Wall Street man A. Palmer Harrison, Painter Price— did they all come from high society? That probably wouldn't be true of the pro football player, What's-His-Name."

"It just happened," Ellery stated, "that Price was born in a Greenwich Village loft. And Valetta came from the slums of Chicago."

They pondered.

"Had three of the four men ever served on the same jury with Valetta?" Darnell asked suddenly.

"No."

"On a TV show?"

"No, Dr. Vreeland."

Miss Wandermere suddenly said, "It isn't anything like that. Am I right, Mr. Queen, that all the facts necessary to solve the puzzle were given to us in your story?"

Ellery chuckled. "I wondered when someone was going to ask that. That's exactly so, Miss Wandermere. There's really no need to ask any questions at all."

"Then I for one need more time," said Mr. Syres. "What

about the rest of you? I suggest we enjoy dinner before we solve Ellery's puzzle."

They ate in silence, deep in thought. Then, one by one, each member's face suddenly lit up. But no one said a word until they were seated in the living room again.

"I see from your looks," Ellery said, "that none of you had any real difficulty with my puzzle."

"It's too bad the President missed this," said Syres, smiling. "He would have loved it! Is everyone ready?"

They all nodded.

"In that case," said Ellery, "which of Valetta's four admirers murdered her?"

"Ladies first," said Dr. Vreeland, nodding to Miss Wandermere.

"The key to the puzzle," said Miss Wandermere, "lies in the fact, Mr. Queen, that you really told us just one thing about Valetta and her four admirers. It follows that whatever she and three of the four men had in common must be related to that thing."

"Very true," said Ellery. "And what was that thing?"

Darnell grinned. "What thinking about the President's visit here tonight must have brought to your mind when we asked for a puzzle. Their names."

> Now it's time for YOU to be The Reader as Detective.
>
> Who murdered Valetta Van Buren? Remember this: *Three* of the four men had something in common with Valetta. That thing was their *names*. It was the *fourth* man who killed her! So—who do you think murdered Valetta Van Buren? Was it John Thrushbottom Taylor, A. Palmer Harrison, Leonardo Price, or Biff Wilson?
>
> Read on to see if you are right!

"You named the movie star Valetta Van Buren," said Syres. "*Van Buren—the name of a President of the United States.*"

"Then Playboy John Thrushbottom Taylor the Third," said Dr. Vreeland. "You hid that one, Queen! But of course Taylor is the name of a President of the United States, too—Zachary Taylor."

"And the Wall Street man, A. Palmer Harrison," the lawyer said. "Harrison—William Henry Harrison was a President of the United States. Benjamin Harrison was a President, too."

"And professional football player Biff Wilson," said Miss Wandermere. "That 'Biff' was mastery, Mr. Queen. But—of course, Wilson, for Woodrow Wilson."

"And that leaves just one character whose name," said Syres, "is not the name of a President—Leonardo Price. So Price, the artist, murdered Valetta. You almost had me fooled, Queen. Taylor, Van Buren, Harrison! That was tricky—picking the names of the less well-known Presidents."

"You could hardly expect me to name one of my characters Eisenhower," grinned Ellery. "Which reminds me—here's to our absent President. May he turn out to be the next member of the Puzzle Club!"

I. The Reader as Detective

Read each question below. Then write the letter of the correct answer to each question. Remember, the symbol next to each question identifies the *kind* of reading skill that particular question helps you to develop.

1. Leonardo Price was a

   a. poet.

   b. Wall Street success.

   c. painter.

2. The President did not attend the meeting of the Puzzle Club because

   a. he did not receive the invitation on time.

   b. he hated mysteries.

   c. a problem in the Middle East had come up.

3. Ellery agreed that the Club could "disregard the possibility" that Valetta and three of the men were of the same age. Which of the following expressions best defines the word *disregard?*

   a. pay no attention to
   b. ask questions about
   c. agree with

4. According to Ellery, which of the following happened *last?*

   a. Valetta took a trip to New York.
   b. Valetta turned down four proposals of marriage.
   c. Valetta sent Ellery a letter.

5. Three of the four suspects in the mystery

   a. were born in Chicago.
   b. served on the same jury.
   c. had the last name of a president.

6. An emergency caused the President to "cancel his flight." What is the meaning of the word *cancel?*

   a. begin   *b.* continue   *c.* call off

7. Which one of the following statements expresses an opinion?

   a. You are certain to like the next story you read by Ellery Queen.
   b. Leonardo Price murdered Valetta Van Buren.
   c. Mr. Syres was the founder of the Puzzle Club.

8. Which one of the following sentences from the story suggests that each member of the Club solved the mystery?

   a. Then all we have to do is find out what they had in common.
   b. They ate in silence, deep in thought.
   c. Then, one by one, each member's face suddenly lit up.

9. The newest member of the Puzzle Club was

   a. Ellery Queen.   *c.* Dr. Vreeland.
   b. Emmy Wandermere.

10. This story is mainly about

    a. the way in which Valetta Van Buren was murdered.

    b. some presidents of the United States.

    c. a mystery which is solved by the members of the Puzzle Club.

II. On the Trail of Story Elements

Answer the questions below. They will provide further review of the following story elements: setting, characterization, and plot.

11. What is the setting of "The President Regrets"?

    a. an apartment in New York

    b. a movie studio in Hollywood

    c. the President's office in Washington

12. Which statement best characterizes Ellery?

    a. He was poor at solving mysteries.

    b. He was a close friend of the President.

    c. He was very skillful at making up clever mysteries.

13. Which sentence best describes Valetta Van Buren?

    a. She was a movie star who became terrified by a death threat.

    b. She was a screen star who was not very glamorous.

    c. She received a death threat, which she ignored.

14. Identify the event which occurred first in the plot of the story.

    a. Syres asked Ellery to help the Puzzle Club.

    b. Dr. Vreeland realized that it was necessary to discover what three of the four men had in common.

    c. The members of the Puzzle Club ate dinner.

15. Which of the following facts is *most important* in the plot of "The President Regrets"?

    a. Biff Wilson was a football player.

    b. The murderer did not have the last name of a president.

    c. It was decided to ask the President to apply for membership in the Club.

III. Finding Word Meanings

Now it's time to be a word detective. Listed below are five vocabulary words which appear in "The President Regrets" and five *new* vocabulary words for you to learn. Study the words and their definitions. Then complete the following paragraphs by using each vocabulary word only *once*.

		page
ordeal	a very difficult or painful experience	65
penthouse	an apartment on the top floor or roof of a building	65
glamorous	fascinating; exciting	66
professional	a person who works in a particular occupation for pay	67
rejected	turned down; not accepted	67
colossal	very large; enormous	
industrious	hardworking	
recognition	the act of being recognized or known	
assurance	certainty	
pursue	to follow	

How would you like to be a writer of mysteries? It sounds like exciting, even __16__ work. You might gain fame and __17__. You might even become a huge, or __18__, success.

But remember this before you think about moving to a fancy __19__. Becoming a successful, well-paid __20__ in the writing field isn't easy. There is no certainty, or __21__, that your stories will be accepted. It is hard to ignore the pain of having your work turned down, or __22__. It can be a very unpleasant __23__. Still, if you are hardworking, or __24__, you may want to __25__ a career as a mystery writer.

IV. Telling About the Case

Suppose you wanted to see if a friend could guess the solution to Ellery's puzzle. Explain what important facts you would have to include when you told your friend the mystery.

First make a list of the items you wish to include. Then number then in the order in which you think they should appear. Use this outline as a guide in presenting the mystery.

"His shirt sleeves were rolled up. On his left forearm, which had fallen across his chest, there was a small red spot. As I watched, the spot grew bigger and redder."

Introducing
Ellery's Mom

by Margaret Austin

Mom is short and kind of chunky and looks like she might belong to the Garden Club, which she does. I guess it's because we've known her all our lives that we don't think of her as Katherine Sanders MacKay. But she's got her name on as many mystery books as Agatha Christie.

To Dad she's just "Kate," and to us five kids, "Mom." To the town busybodies for many years she was "that woman who neglects those poor kids, my, I don't know how the doctor stands it!" But Mom didn't look at it that way. She said that making our own peanut butter sandwiches taught us self-reliance and independence. And that after being around an office all day, it relaxed Dad to come home to a place that was lived-in.

As for Dad, I think he liked Mom being a writer. When he was called out at night, she'd get up and write a few hundred words. Then when he got home, they'd drink coffee and discuss their cases.

Of course, sometimes I think Mom carried this mystery business too far. It's convenient for a mystery writer to have a doctor right there. But it kind of rocked Dad to have her ask, right in the middle of eating scrambled eggs, "Where would you knife a person to have instantaneous death and very little blood?" or suddenly she'd come out with something like, "I think I'll freeze him to death." I mean it isn't normal conversation.

As for me, I'm Ellery—named after Ellery Queen, the mystery writer. Mostly everyone calls me "Ray." I'm not the Ellery type.

Anyway, by the day James Griggs, the chemistry teacher, died, Mom was something of a celebrity around Maplecrest, where we live.

Once, I asked Mom if she couldn't get more inspiration living in a city where more exciting things happened than in Maplecrest, which took a sleeping pill sometime in the 1880's.

"My goodness, no!" she replied. "What you need for inspiration is not excitement—it's character. City dwellers don't know five people as well as I know most of the people around here."

Which brings me back to the day Mr. Griggs, the chemistry teacher, died. And why I needed to talk to Mom.

I'd been at the baseball tryouts after school. So the halls were deserted when I went to my locker. I was on my way there when Miss Dean came out of the chem lab. She turned at the door and called, "I'll see you tomorrow night at eight, then?" She listened briefly to someone inside the lab. Then she added, "No. I'm sure he doesn't suspect anything. It would be terrible if he did!"

She walked briskly down the hall, stuffing a bright card into an envelope as she came. I wished I could have disappeared into the locker or gone into orbit or something. But I just stood there and said, real original-like, "Hello, Miss Dean."

Sure, it startled her, but she recovered quickly. She waved at me and went on. I couldn't have been at my locker for more than five minutes when I heard Mr. Griggs scream. It was a terrible scream, along with a crash of glass—then silence.

Well, naturally, I raced down the hall. Even so, I wasn't the first one there. The principal, Mr. Wilson, dashed through the west door and beat me to the lab by a good thirty feet.

"Stay back! Stay back, boy!" he yelled, so I parked in the doorway.

Mr. Wilson kneeled on the floor around a mess of broken test tubes. He blocked the view, but those were certainly Mr. Griggs's long skinny legs. His feet flopped out with one foot pointing to me and the other pointing to the open window across the room. Just looking at those feet, you knew he was dead.

I stood there. Then old Smitty, the janitor who's been with the school for the last century, tapped my shoulder. I moved into the room to let him in.

The principal stood up. He pulled a handkerchief from his pocket, and wiped it across his forehead. Now I could see Mr. Griggs clearly. You'd think with Dad being a doctor and Mom writing about death all the time, that I'd be hardened. But it doesn't look the same in real life as it does in books.

Nobody ever called Mr. Griggs handsome. His eyes kind of bulged—maybe from looking at too many Bunsen burners. A couple of weeks ago, when Miss Dean started being seen in quiet corners with him, I sure wondered why.

Sprawled there on the lab floor, he was even less appealing. One thing really fascinated me, though. His shirt sleeves were rolled up. On his left forearm, which had fallen across his chest, there was a small red spot. As I watched, the spot grew bigger and redder.

"Smitty," Mr. Wilson said, "clean up this broken stuff before someone is cut. He's dead—probably his heart. But I'll call Doc Morton." Then, noticing me, he added, "His office is right across the street."

"Ray," he went on, almost kindly, "there's nothing we can do. Go on home and try not to think about this."

So I went outside—but not home. Nosirreebob! I went out to the parking lot. Then I circled back through the bushes until I was outside the chem lab window. And was I glad I did! There in the soft earth under the window were footprints. They were blurred. But maybe the police could find a clear one.

It wasn't long till voices came through the lab window. Heart attack all right, Dr. Morton announced. It didn't surprise him one bit, the way Jim Griggs wouldn't listen when he was told to take it easy. Dr. Morton said they'd better notify Police Chief Higgins. There really was nothing for the Chief to do, but he likes to know what's going on around town.

Just then I got careless, and Mr. Wilson saw my red cap above the windowsill. A principal has lots of practice reading the riot act, so I hurried off for home. Besides, I had to talk to Mom!

Mom was working away on the porch. Her pencil moved furiously over a sheet of yellow paper.

"Hello, dear—have a nice day?" The pencil didn't break its flying rhythm.

"Mom, something strange happened this afternoon. Mr. Griggs died."

"Hmm. That's nice, dear." The pencil still flew.

"Mom," I said loudly, "it might be M—U—R—D—E—R!" That stopped the pencil in midair.

"Ray, there hasn't been a murder in Maplecrest since 1858. You've inherited my imagination. But sit down and tell me all about it."

I told her everything, just the way it had happened.

"But Bob Wilson is engaged to Clara Dean, isn't he?"

"That's just it, Mom! Everybody knows he gave her the

ring at Christmas. They're supposed to be married this summer. But for the last couple of weeks she's been sneaking around with Mr. Griggs. And then he dies and Mr. Wilson is right there on the scene!"

"Hmm. What do you think of him, Ellery?" You know she's serious when she starts calling me Ellery.

"For a principal, he's always seemed like a right guy. He was even pretty good about it when he took away my pea-shooter—" Oh, oh, too late! There I stood with a mouth full of feet.

"What's this, young man?" A short lecture followed. Then, with that taken care of, Mom got back to the case.

"I wish they'd called your father," she said. "Old Dr. Morton should have retired years ago. He couldn't tell a heart attack from . . ." Her voice trailed off. Then she got that spark in her eye that she gets when she's finally worked out the solution to a mystery. "Ellery, get your father's *Modern Drug Encyclopedia.*"

She flipped through the pages until she found what she wanted. Then she scribbled a few lines on a sheet of yellow paper and stuck it into her pocket.

"I still don't see. . ." she said to herself. "If he came in the west door, then the footprints . . ." She turned to me. "Were there screens on that window? No! That's it, of course!"

"Got it solved, Mom?" I asked hopefully.

"Absolutely! Stupid of me not to see it immediately. Oh, he was clever! And he would have gotten away with it if you hadn't been there! Come on, we're going to talk to Chief Higgins. You can be sure he won't see it." Then she added generously, "Of course, he doesn't have all the facts, as I do."

Chief Higgins greeted us cheerfully. He and Mom have gotten to know each other pretty well over the years.

"Well, Kate MacKay! This is a pleasant surprise! How's the doctor and the rest of the family?"

With the small talk out of the way, Mom got down to business. "Chief," she said, "I've heard about Jim Griggs's death at the High School this afternoon. Ray was there and I think we might be helpful to you. I don't mean to be poking my nose into your department, but some facts may have been concealed."

Then she told what I'd heard and seen. When Mom finished telling about my part in the case, the Chief looked puzzled. "Yes, that's the way it happened," he said. "But I don't see what you're driving at."

"Well, I didn't see it either, at first," said Mom. "But did you know that Clara Dean is engaged to Bob Wilson? And that she's been seeing Jim Griggs a lot recently. Ellery has seen them together several times. That certainly gives Bob Wilson a reason—and he was right at the scene. From the footprints outside the window, I believe he was standing there when Griggs started screaming. He could have run from there to the chemistry lab faster than Ellery could have run from his locker.

"But that still left the question of how he actually committed the murder. That baffled me, Chief—until Ellery let slip about the principal's taking a peashooter away from him. There you have it! The natives of Borneo use blowguns with poisoned darts. They're effective at far greater distances than Wilson was from Griggs. As soon as Wilson reached the body, he ordered Ellery to stay back *while he removed the dart*. He pocketed it when he removed his handkerchief. You'll find a small hole under Griggs's left arm, I'm sure.

"Oh, yes," she finished, "quinidine was probably the poison used." She took the piece of yellow paper from her pocket and put it on his desk. "As principal, he could easily unlock the nurse's office at night and take all he needed. If the theft were noticed, it would be reported to him, and he'd simply forget it. Quinidine gives the appearance of a heart attack. Another doctor might have been suspicious. But you and I know that Dr. Morton's not what he used to be. That's probably why Bob Wilson called him."

Chief Higgins sat quietly at his desk for several moments. Finally he spoke. "Kate," he said, "for a long time now I've been a great admirer of yours. I've read all your books. Frankly, the hero usually figures out who the murderer is before I do. But this beats anything you ever wrote. It's just as neat as any bit of deduction ever was. My hat's off to you."

Mom sat there beaming.

"In fact," the Chief continued, "it makes me downright ashamed to tell you that it didn't happen that way at all." Then he added generously, "Of course, you don't have all the facts like I do."

Now it's time for YOU to be The Reader as Detective.

What do you think Chief Higgins told Mom? What was his explanation for the "murder" of Mr. Griggs? Read on to see if you are right!

"First, there wasn't anything between Jim Griggs and Clara Dean—except plans for Bob Wilson's surprise birthday party tomorrow night. The whole faculty was in on it. But those two were getting the present for him and handling the details.

"Second, it was Smitty the janitor who made those tracks in the dirt outside the window—while he was washing it.

"Third," the Chief went on, "Jim Griggs did have a problem with his heart—has had it for several years. You're right about the puncture on the arm, though. Made by a wasp. There's your murderer. Griggs crashed around in the lab trying to kill it. The exertion and the excitement, plus the shock from the wasp's sting, set off the heart attack."

Mom and I were kind of quiet all the way home. She took it real hard, and I forgot my own stupid mistake, worrying about her. When we reached the front porch, Mom dropped into our old-fashioned swing and sat there. I sat on the steps and said nothing.

Dad came home soon. Seeing me sitting there he asked, "Why the gloom?"

I told him the whole embarrassing story. When I got to the part about the poison, he said, "I wish she had called me. It would take a harpoon to carry a deadly load of quinidine."

We both looked down to the end of the porch where Mom still sat in the swing.

Her eyes had that far-away look they always get when she's plotting a new novel.

"Who do you suppose," she asked softly, "knew about Jim Griggs's heart condition and wanted him out of the way badly enough to leave a wasp in the chemistry laboratory?"

I. The Reader as Detective

Read each question below. Then write the letter of the correct answer to each question. Remember, the symbol next to each question identifies the *kind* of reading skill that particular question helps you to develop.

1. Mr. MacKay was a

    a. writer.   *b.* teacher.   *c.* doctor.

2. Ellery stated that Maplecrest "took a sleeping pill sometime in the 1880's." We may infer from this statement that Ellery thought that

    a. Maplecrest was a very exciting place in which to live.
    b. few exciting things happened in Maplecrest.
    c. most people had trouble falling asleep in Maplecrest.

3. After Ray overheard voices through the lab window, he

    a. rushed home.
    b. said hello to Miss Dean.
    c. went to his locker.

4. "City dwellers don't know five people as well as I know most of the people around here," said Kate MacKay. City *dwellers* are people who

    a. write about the city.
    b. live in the city.
    c. take vacations in the city.

5. Mom thought that the principal, Mr. Wilson,

    a. murdered the chemistry teacher.
    b. was jealous of Mr. Griggs.
    c. both of the above.

6. Which one of the following statements expresses an opinion?

    a. There were footprints in the earth near the chemistry lab window.
    b. Mystery stories are more enjoyable than love stories.
    c. Mr. Griggs had a red spot on his left arm.

7. Mom told Ray, "You've inherited my imagination." What is the meaning of the word *inherited?*

    a. lost   *b.* forgotten   *c.* received

8. According to Chief Higgins, Mr. Griggs was killed by

    a. a wasp.   *b.* a dart.   *c.* the janitor.

9. Dad stated, "It would take a harpoon to carry a deadly load of quinidine." This suggests that

    a. quinidine is usually carried in harpoons.

    b. quinidine is a very powerful poison.

    c. quinidine is not a very powerful poison.

10. The story is mainly about

    a. a typical day at a high school.

    b. a mystery writer who incorrectly "solves" a crime.

    c. a surprise birthday party for Bob Wilson.

II. On the Trail of Story Elements

Another important story element is **tone**. The tone of a story is the overall *mood* that the writing creates. For example, the tone of a comedy is humorous, while a tragedy is serious in tone. Tone also refers to the way an author *views* his or her characters or material. What is the author's *attitude*, or tone? Is it serious, bitter, sympathetic, or amused?

Answer the questions below. Questions 11-13 deal with tone. Questions 14 and 15 refer to plot.

11. The tone of "Introducing Ellery's Mom" is

    a. serious.   *b.* humorous.   *c.* terrifying.

12. Which word best describes the author's attitude toward her characters?

    a. bitter   *b.* sad   *c.* amused

13. Mom's theory about the murder proved to be incorrect. What is the author's attitude toward her?

    a. angry   *b.* sympathetic   *c.* unsympathetic

14. Which of the following is most important to the plot of the story?

    a. a Bunsen burner in the chemistry laboratory

    b. a new novel Mom was writing

    c. Bob Wilson's surprise birthday party

15. Which event in the plot happened last?

    a. The principal found Mr. Griggs in the laboratory.

    b. Mom and Ellery visited Chief Higgins.

    c. Smitty tapped Ellery on the shoulder and moved into the room.

III. Finding Word Meanings

Now it's time to be a word detective. Below are ten words which appear in "Introducing Ellery's Mom." Study the words and the definitions beside them. Then complete the following paragraphs by using each word only *once.*

		page
self-reliance	confidence in one's own ability	75
instantaneous	in an instant; very sudden; immediate	75
celebrity	a famous person	76
inspiration	a sudden, brilliant idea	76
lecture	a talk on a particular subject	79
scribbled	wrote quickly	79
baffled	puzzled	80
deduction	finding out through reasoning	80
faculty	the teachers of a school	81
exertion	effort	81

Last Sunday, I went to hear a __16__ given by Professor Hugo Stumpem. Professor Stumpem is a __17__ who is famous for his mystery stories. They are based on reasoning, or __18__ . The professor is also on the __19__ of the College of Knowledge.

I __20__ a few notes on a pad while Professor Stumpem spoke. According to Professor Stumpem, "Almost anyone can write a mystery which will leave the reader __21__ and confused. However, it is not enough simply to sit around and hope for __22__ for a story. Good ideas do not come suddenly in an __23__ fashion. They are the result of __24__ , or hard work. If you do not write an outstanding story at once, don't be discouraged. You can do it! Confidence, or __25__ , is important."

IV. Telling About the Case

A. Katherine MacKay and Chief Higgins each offered an explanation for the death of Mr. Griggs. Discuss the theory that each presented and show how Mom and the Chief came to different conclusions.

B. At the beginning of the story, Ellery noticed Miss Dean "stuffing a bright card into an envelope" as she walked down the hall. Show that this is an important clue that Ellery overlooked.

C. At the conclusion of the story, Mom asked: "Who do you suppose knew about Jim Griggs's heart condition and wanted him out of the way badly enough to leave a wasp in the chemistry laboratory?" What does this suggest Mom is planning to do?

A Retrieved Reformation

by O. Henry

A guard came to the prison shoe shop where Jimmy Valentine was carefully fixing a pair of heels.

"The warden wants to see you, Valentine," he said.

He led him to the front office where the warden was waiting.

"Now, Valentine," said the warden, "you'll be getting out in the morning. Here's a word of advice. Stand up and make a man of yourself. You're not a bad fellow, at heart. Stop cracking safes, and live straight."

"Me?" said Jimmy, in surprise. "Why, I never cracked a safe in my life."

"Oh, no," said the warden. "Of course not. Let's see, now. How was it that you happened to get sent up on that Springfield job? Was it simply a case of a mean old jury that had it in for you?"

"Me?" said Jimmy, looking virtuous. "Why, warden, I never was in Springfield in my life."

The warden smiled and shook his head. "Take him back, Cronin," he said. "Fix him up with some outgoing clothes. Unlock him at seven in the morning. Better think over what I said, Valentine."

At a quarter past seven the next morning, Jimmy stood in the warden's outer office. The clerk handed him a railroad ticket and a ten-dollar bill. The warden shook hands and said good-bye, and Jimmy Valentine, Number 9762, walked out into the sunshine.

Jimmy headed straight for a restaurant. There he tasted the first sweet joys of liberty. The prize ingredients were a broiled chicken and chocolate pie. After this refreshing meal, he walked leisurely to the railroad station. He tossed a quarter into the hat of a blind man sitting by the door. Then he boarded his train.

Three hours later, Jimmy arrived in a little town near the state line. He went to a diner and shook hands with his old friend, Mike, who was standing alone behind the counter.

"Glad to see you, Jimmy," said Mike. "Feeling all right?"

"Fine," said Jimmy. "Have you got my key?"

Jimmy took the key and went upstairs. He unlocked the door of a room at the rear. Everything was just as he had left it. There on the floor were still Ben Price's collar buttons. They had been torn from that famous detective's shirt when they had overpowered Jimmy to arrest him.

Jimmy pulled a folding bed out from the wall. Sliding back a panel in the wall, he dragged out a dusty suitcase. He opened it and gazed fondly at the finest set of burglar's tools in the East. It was a complete set, made of the hardest steel. There were the best drills, punches and clamps, as well as a few special tools that Jimmy had invented himself. All together, they had cost him over fifteen hundred dollars to have made at a place where they quietly handle such things.

In half an hour, Jimmy went downstairs. He was dressed in a tasteful and well-fitting suit, and, in his hand, he carried his dusted and cleaned suitcase.

"Going out on a job?" asked Mike softly.

"Why, Mike," said Jimmy smiling, "I don't understand what you mean. I'm a salesman." He pointed to his suitcase. "I work for the New York Frazzled Wheat Biscuit and Crackers Company."

Both men burst out laughing. Jimmy waved good-bye and headed out the door.

Less than a week later, there was a neat job of safe-cracking done in Richmond, Indiana. Twelve hundred dollars was taken, with no clue left behind. Two weeks after that, a new, improved, burglarproof safe was opened like a cheese to the tune of twenty-five hundred dollars. That began to interest the police greatly. Then an old-fashioned bank safe in Jefferson City was cracked. Seven thousand dollars was stolen. The losses were now high enough to bring the matter to Ben Price's attention.

He compared notes on the robberies and observed a remarkable similarity in the methods of the burglar. Then he visited the scenes of the crimes.

"That's Jimmy Valentine's work," he was heard to say. "He's resumed business again. Look at the knob—pulled out as easy as tugging up a radish in wet weather. He's got the only clamps that can do it. And look how clean those tumblers were punched out! Jimmy never has to drill more than one hole. Yes, I guess it's Mr. Valentine I want, all right."

Ben Price knew Jimmy's habits. He had learned them while working on the Springfield case. He put everything else aside and took up the trail.

One afternoon, Jimmy and his suitcase climbed out of a railroad car in the little town of Elmore, Arkansas. Looking very fit and well dressed, Jimmy marched briskly down the main street toward the hotel.

A young woman crossed the street. She passed him at the corner and opened the door of the Elmore Bank. Jimmy Valentine looked into her eyes, forgot what he was, and became another man. She lowered her eyes and turned slightly red. Young men of Jimmy's style and looks were rare in Elmore.

Jimmy stopped a boy who was hanging about on the steps of the bank. He began to ask him questions about the town, tossing him dimes from time to time. By and by the young woman came out. Trying hard not to notice the young man with the suitcase, she went on her way.

"Isn't that Miss Polly Simpson?" asked Jimmy.

"Naw," said the boy. "She's Annabel Adams. Her pa owns this bank. What'd you come to Elmore for? Is that a gold watchchain? I'm going to get a bulldog. Got any more dimes?"

Jimmy went to the Planter's Hotel. There he signed in as Ralph D. Spencer and rented a room. He leaned on the desk and told his story to the clerk. He said he had come to Elmore to look for a spot to go into business. "How is the shoe business now, in this town?" he asked. He had thought of the shoe business. "Was there an opening?"

The clerk was impressed with the clothes and manner of Jimmy. "Yes," he said, "there ought to be a good opening in the shoe line. As a matter of fact," he continued, "there isn't a real shoe store in the town. The general stores handle them all. Hope you decide to settle in Elmore, Mr. Spencer. You'll find it a pleasant town to live in, and the people real friendly."

Mr. Spencer thought he would stop over in town a few days and look over the situation. No, the clerk needn't call the boy. He would carry the suitcase up himself; it was rather heavy.

And so Mr. Ralph D. Spencer arose from the ashes of Jimmy Valentine—ashes left by the soaring flame of a sudden attack of love. He became a new man. He stayed in Elmore, opened a shoe store and managed to sustain himself with a good run of trade.

Socially he was also a success and made many friends. He also accomplished the wish of his heart. He met Miss Annabel Adams, and became more and more captivated by her charms.

At the termination of a year, the situation of Mr. Ralph D. Spencer was this: He had won the respect of everyone in town, his shoe store was flourishing, and he and Annabel Adams were engaged to be married in two weeks. Mr. Adams, the prominent country banker, liked Spencer, and Annabel's pride in him almost equaled her affection.

One day Jimmy sat down in his room. He wrote this letter which he mailed to the safe address of one of his old friends in St. Louis.

Dear Old Pal:

I want you to be at Sullivan's place in Little Rock, next Wednesday night. Make it at nine o'-clock. I want you to wind up some matters for me. Also, I want to give you a little present. It's my kit of tools which I know you'll be glad to get. You couldn't duplicate a set like that for fifteen hundred dollars. Say, Billy, I've quit the old business—a year ago. I've got a nice store. I'm making an honest living, and I'm going to marry the finest woman on earth two weeks from now. It's the only life, Billy—the straight one. I wouldn't touch a dollar of another man's money now for a million. After I get married, I'm going to sell out and go West, where there won't be so much danger of having old scores brought against me. I tell you, Billy, she's an angel. She believes in me, and I wouldn't do another crooked thing for the whole world. Be sure to be at Sullivan's, for I must see you. I'll bring the tools along with me.

> Your old friend,
> Jimmy

On the Monday night after Jimmy wrote this letter, Ben Price slipped quietly into Elmore. He hung about town until he found out what he wanted to know. From the drugstore across the street from Spencer's Shoe Store, he got a good look at Ralph D. Spencer.

"Going to marry the banker's daughter are you, Jimmy?" said Ben softly to himself. "Well, I don't know about that!"

The next morning, Jimmy had breakfast with the Adamses. He said he was going to Little Rock that day to order his wedding suit and to buy something nice for Annabel. That would be the first time he had left town since he came to Elmore. It had been more than a year since he had pulled a job, and he thought he could safely venture out.

After breakfast, quite a family party went downtown together. There were Mr. Adams, Annabel and Jimmy. They were joined by Annabel's married sister with her two little girls, aged five and nine. They came by the hotel where Jimmy still stayed. He ran up to his room and brought down his suitcase. Then they went on to the bank. From there, Dolph Gibson was going to drive him in a carriage to the railroad station.

They all went into the banking room with its high, carved oak railing. Jimmy was included, for Mr. Adams' future son-in-law was welcome anywhere. The clerks were glad to say hello to the good-looking, agreeable young man who was going to marry Annabel.

Jimmy set his suitcase down. Annabel's heart was bubbling with happiness and high spirits. She put on Jimmy's hat and picked up his suitcase. She put it down quickly.

"My, Ralph," she said, "how heavy it is. It feels like it's full of gold bricks."

"Lot of metal shoehorns in there that I'm going to return," said Jimmy, cooly. "I thought I'd bring them down my-self and save the shipping charges."

The Elmore Bank had just put in a new safe and vault. Mr. Adams was very proud of it and insisted that everyone see it. The vault was a small one, but it had a brand new door. It locked with three heavy steel bolts, and had a time-lock.

With a big smile, Mr. Adams explained how it worked to Mr. Spencer, who listened politely. The two children, May and Agatha, were delighted by the shining metal and the funny clocks and knobs.

While this was taking place, Ben Price dropped in. He leaned on his elbow and looked casually between the railing. He told the teller that he didn't want anything, that he was just waiting for a man he knew.

Suddenly there were loud screams and a commotion. Without being perceived by the elders, May, the nine-year-old girl, in a spirit of play, had shut Agatha in the vault. She had then dropped the bolts and turned the knob on the lock as she had seen Mr. Adams do.

The old banker rushed to the handle and tugged at it for a moment.

"The door can't be opened," he groaned. "The clock hasn't been wound nor the combination set."

Mr. Adams raised his trembling hand. "Agatha," he called, as loudly as he could, "listen to me."

During the silence that followed, they could hear the faint sound of the child wildly shrieking in terror from within the dark vault.

"My child," wailed the mother, "she'll die of fright! Open the door! Break it open! Can't anyone do something!"

"There isn't a man nearer than Little Rock who can open that door," said Mr. Adams in a shaky voice. "Spencer, what shall we do? That child—she can't stand it very long in there. There isn't enough air."

Agatha's mother, frantic now, beat the door of the vault with her hands. Somebody wildly suggested dynamite. An-nabel turned to Jimmy. Her large eyes were filled with an-guish, but not yet with despair.

"Can't you do something, Ralph?—Try, won't you?"

He looked at her with a funny, soft smile on his lips and in his keen eyes.

"Annabel," he said, "give me that rose you are wearing, will you?"

Hardly believing that she had heard him right, she unpinned the bud from her dress, and placed it in his hand. Jimmy stuffed it into his vest pocket, threw off his coat, and rolled up his shirt-sleeves. With that act, Ralph D. Spencer passed away and Jimmy Valentine took his place.

"Get away from that door, all of you!" he ordered.

He set his suitcase on the table and opened it flat. From that time on, he seemed to be unaware that anyone else was there. He laid out the shining tools swiftly and neatly, whistling softly to himself as he always did when at work. The others, silent and unmoving, watched him, as though under a spell.

In a minute, Jimmy's favorite pet drill was cutting smoothly into the steel door. In ten minutes—breaking his own record—he threw back the bolts and opened the door.

There lay Agatha on the floor, breathing weakly, but safe.

Jimmy Valentine put on his coat and walked beyond the railing towards the front door. As he went, he thought he heard a dim voice calling out to him, "Ralph!" But he never stopped.

At the door, a big man stood in his way.

"Hello, Ben!" said Jimmy, still with his strange smile. "Got around at last, have you? Well, let's go. I don't know that it makes much difference now."

And then Ben Price acted rather strangely.

> Now it's time for YOU to be The Reader as Detective.
>
> How did Ben Price act strangely? What do you think he said to Jimmy Valentine? Read on to see if you are right!

"Guess you're mistaken, Mr. Spencer," he said. "Don't believe I know you. Your carriage is waiting for you, isn't it?"

And Ben Price turned and walked down the street.

I. The Reader as Detective

Read each question below. Then write the letter of the correct answer to each question. Remember, the symbol next to each question identifies the *kind* of reading skill that particular question helps you to develop.

1. Jimmy's suitcase was filled with

    a. tools.   *b.* shoes.   *c.* shoehorns.

2. Jimmy's letter stated that he

    a. knew that Ben Price was following him.

    b. was planning to rob a bank.

    c. was going to be married.

3. After Ben Price visited the scenes of the crimes, he realized that Jimmy had "resumed business." Which word or expression best defines the word *resumed*?

    a. finished
    b. started again
    c. finally found

4. Which one of the following statements expresses an opinion?

    a. Jimmy will probably return to a life of crime one day.
    b. Jimmy fell in love with Annabel "at first sight."
    c. As Ralph D. Spencer, Jimmy opened a shoe store.

5. What could be found on the floor of Jimmy's room?

    a. blood stains
    b. collar buttons
    c. a heavy metal safe

6. Which happened last?

    a. Jimmy asked Annabel for a rose.
    b. Ben Price told the teller he was waiting for a man he knew.
    c. Jimmy rented a room at the Planter's Hotel.

7. Mr. Adams owned a bank in

    a. Springfield.
    b. Little Rock.
    c. Elmore.

8. Jimmy said it was not possible to "duplicate" a set of burglar tools like his for fifteen hundred dollars. Which expression best defines the word *duplicate*?

    a. make an exact copy   *c.* search everywhere
    b. lose carelessly

9. Probably, Ben Price didn't arrest Jimmy because

    a. Price wasn't certain that it really was Jimmy.
    b. Price thought that it would upset Mr. Adams, the banker.
    c. Price realized that Jimmy had reformed.

10. Which one of the following would make the best title for this story?

    a. Love Changes a Man
    b. Safe Cracker Pulls Many Jobs
    c. Girl Locked in Safe

II. On the Trail of Story Elements

Another important story element is **style**. Style refers to the *way in which a story is written.* The special way an author uses language determines that author's style. An author's style, for example, may be poetic or witty, or it may feature many long, descriptive passages.

Answer the questions below. Questions 11–13 deal with style. Questions 14 and 15 refer to plot and characterization.

11. Judging from this story, it is fair to say that O. Henry's style

    a. aims at frightening or terrifying the reader.
    b. features an ending intended to surprise.
    c. makes the reader feel sadness or sorrow.

12. At the beginning of the story, Jimmy Valentine "tossed a quarter into the hat of a blind man sitting by the door." This is O. Henry's way of indicating that

    a. although Jimmy had spent time in prison, he was very wealthy.
    b. although Jimmy was a safecracker, he was good at heart.
    c. Jimmy knew that Ben Price was watching him.

13. Which group of words best describes O. Henry's style?

    a. light, entertaining, amusing
    b. serious, solemn, complicated
    c. bitter, humorless, heavy

14. Which one of the following played the *most important* part in the plot of the story?

    a. The warden gave Jimmy some words of advice.
    b. May shut Agatha in the vault.
    c. Jimmy sent a letter to a friend in St. Louis.

15. Which statement correctly describes how Jimmy's character changed during the course of the story?

    a. He changed from a criminal to a salesman for the New York Frazzled Wheat Biscuit and Crackers Company.

    b. He changed from a bank robber to a responsible business-man.

    c. He did not really change at all.

III. Finding Word Meanings

Now it's time to be a word detective. Below are ten words which appear in "A Retrieved Reformation." Study the words and the definitions beside them. Then complete the following paragraphs by using each word only *once*. The completed passage will provide information about O. Henry's style.

		page
virtuous	good; moral	86
ingredients	parts	87
refreshing	delightful; able to refresh	87
similarity	quality of being alike	88
sustain	to endure; experience; support	89
captivated	fascinated; charmed	89
prominent	well-known or important	89
termination	ending	89
perceived	seen; observed	91
anguish	great grief or pain	91

For more than 75 years, the stories of O. Henry have charmed and __16__ readers. What are the __17__ that make his stories so popular?

To begin with, the stories are entertaining and delightful; that is, they are very __18__ . Not all of O. Henry's characters are honest, good, or __19__ , but they are never really evil. They seldom endure, or __20__ , great pain and __21__ . Rather they may be seen, or __22__ , as victims of fate's twists.

All of O. Henry's stories are alike in one special way. What is this key __23__ ? It is the "surprise" ending found at the conclusion, or __24__ , of each story. The "surprise" ending is the most important, or __25__ , feature of O. Henry's writing.

IV. Telling About the Case

A. This story is entitled "A Retrieved Reformation." The word *retrieved* means recovered, saved, found, or set right. A *reformation* means a change for the better, or improvement. Explain the meaning of the title.

B. When Jimmy saw Ben Price at the bank, he said: "Hello, Ben! Got around at last, have you? Well, let's go. I don't know that it makes much difference now." What did Jimmy mean when he stated that it didn't make "much difference now"?

C. At the conclusion of the story, Ben Price decided to let Jimmy Valentine go. Why do you think he did this? Explain why you agree or disagree with his decision. It will be interesting to see how many classmates agree with you—and which point of view proves most popular.

Phut Phat
Concentrates

by Lilian Jackson Braun

Phut Phat knew, at an early age, that humans were
inferior. They were unable to see in the dark. They
ate and drank unthinkable food. And they had only five
senses. The two who lived with Phut Phat, the cat, could not
even communicate their thoughts without using words.

For more than a year, Phut Phat had been attempting to
introduce *his* system of communication. But his two pupils
had made little progress. At dinner time he would sit in a
corner, *concentrating*. Suddenly they would say, "Time to
feed the cat," as if it were *their* own idea.

Their ability to grasp Phut Phat's messages extended only
to the necessities of daily living. Beyond that, nothing ever
got through to them. And it seemed unlikely that they would
ever increase their powers.

Nevertheless, life was comfortable enough for Phut Phat.
It was a fashionable part of the city in which he lived. His
home was a three-story brick house furnished with thick rugs
and tall pieces of furniture from which he could look down
on questionable visitors.

Phut Phat was a Siamese cat. His coat was finer than ermine, and his slanted eyes brimmed with a mysterious blue.
The pair who lived with Phut Phat were identified in his mind
as One and Two. It was One who supplied the comforts—beef

on weekdays, liver on Sunday, and a warm cuddle now and then.

Two, on the other hand, was valued chiefly for entertainment. He said very little. But he jingled keys at the end of a shiny chain and swung them back and forth for Phut Phat's amusement. And every morning in the dressing room he swished a necktie in arcs, while Phut Phat leaped and grabbed with his pearly claws.

One Sunday, Phut Phat sensed a disturbing change in the household's routine. The Sunday papers were usually scattered all over the library floor for him to shred with his claws. Today they were stacked neatly on the desk. Furniture was rearranged. The house was filled with flowers, which he was not allowed to chew. All day long One was nervous, and Two was too busy to play. A stranger in a white coat arrived and set up glasses. When Phut Phat went to investigate the scent of shrimp and smoked oysters in the kitchen, the maid shooed him away.

Phut Phat seemed to be in everyone's way. Finally he was deposited in his wire cage on the fire escape. There he watched sparrows in the garden below until his stomach felt empty. Then he howled to come indoors.

He found One at her dressing table. She was fussing with her hair. She was unaware that he was hungry. He hopped lightly to the table. He sat erect among the sparkling bottles, and stiffened his tail. He fastened his blue eyes on One's forehead. Then he concentrated—and *concentrated*—and *concentrated*. It was never easy to communicate with One. Her mind hopped about like a sparrow. Phut Phat had to strain every nerve to convey his meaning.

Suddenly One darted a look in his direction. The thought had *finally* come to her.

"Oh, John," she called to Two, "would you ask Millie to feed Phuffy? I forgot his dinner until this very minute. It's after five o'clock, and I haven't fixed my hair yet. You'd better put your jacket on. People will start coming soon. And please tell Howard to light the candles. You might stack some records on the stereo, too. No, wait a minute. Millie is still working in the kitchen. Would you feed Phuffy yourself? Just give him a slice of cold roast."

At this Phut Phat stared at One and concentrated hard, very hard.

"Oh, John, I forgot," One corrected. "It's Sunday, and he should have liver. Cut it in long strips the way he likes it. *Please*, John, feed Phuffy now. He's staring at me and making my head ache."

Phut Phat scarcely had time to swallow his meal and wash his face before people started to arrive. It was a large party, and Phut Phat observed that very few of the guests knew how to pay their respects to a cat. Some talked nonsense to him in a false voice. Others made startling movements in his direction or, worse still, tried to pick him up.

There was one knowledgeable guest, however, who was different. He was a man who leaned heavily on a shiny silver stick. Standing at a respectful distance, he slowly held out his hand with one finger extended. Phut Phat twitched his whiskers in polite acknowledgment.

"You are a living sculpture," said the man.

"That's Phut Phat," said One. She had pushed through the crowded room toward the fireplace. "He's the head of our household."

"He is obviously a champion," said the man with the shiny cane. He addressed his hostess in the same dignified manner that had charmed Phut Phat.

"Yes, he could probably win a few ribbons if we wanted to enter him in shows. But he's strictly a pet. He never goes out except in his cage on the fire escape."

"A cage? That's a splendid idea," said the man. "I should like to have one for my own cat. May I inspect his cage before I leave?"

"Of course. It's just outside the library window."

"You have a most attractive house."

"Thank you. You'll notice we have nothing breakable. When a Siamese leaps through the air, he recognizes no obstacles."

"Indeed, I have noticed you collect Georgian silver," the man said. "You have some fine examples."

"Apparently you know silver. Your cane is a rare piece."

"Yes." He hobbled a step or two.

"Would you like to see my silver collection downstairs in the dining room?" asked One.

At this point, Phut Phat was aware that the conversation no longer centered on him. He jumped down from the chair and stalked out of the room. He went upstairs to the guest room, where he went to sleep.

After this upset in the household routine, Phut Phat needed several days to catch up on his rest. Therefore, the following week was a sleepy blur. But soon it was Sunday again, with liver for breakfast, Sunday papers scattered over the floor, and everyone sitting around being pleasant.

"Phuffy! Don't roll on those newspapers," said One. "John, can't you see the ink rubs off on his fur?"

"Maybe he'd like to go outside in his cage and get some sun."

"That reminds me, dear. Who was that charming man with the silver cane at our party? I didn't catch his name."

"I don't know," said Two. "I thought he was someone you invited."

"Well, he wasn't. He must have come with one of the other guests. At any rate, he was interested in getting a cage like ours for his own cat. And did I tell you the Hendersons have two Burmese kittens? They want us to go over and see them next Sunday."

That Sunday evening, One and Two went out to see the Burmese kittens. Phut Phat was served an early dinner, and soon afterward he fell asleep on the sofa.

When the telephone rang and awakened him, it was dark and he was alone. He raised his head and chattered at the telephone until it stopped its noise. Then he went back to sleep, chin on paw.

The second time the telephone started ringing, Phut Phat stood up and scolded it. He arched his body and made a question mark with his tail. Then he hopped on the desk and spent quite some time chewing on a leather bookmark. After that he felt thirsty. He headed toward the powder room for a drink.

No lights were burning, and no moonlight came through the windows. Yet he moved through the dark rooms with assurance.

Phut Phat was lapping water when something caused him to raise his head and listen. His tail froze. Sparrows in the backyard? Rain on the fire escape? There was silence again.

He lowered his head and resumed his drinking.

A second time he was alerted. Something was happening that was not routine. His tail bushed like a squirrel's. With his whiskers full of alarm, he stepped noiselessly into the hall, peering toward the library.

Someone was on the fire escape. Something was at the library window.

Petrified, he watched. The window opened and a dark figure slipped into the room. Phut Phat sprang to the top of a tall dresser.

There, on his high perch, able to look down on the scene, he felt safe. But was it enough to feel safe? His ancestors had been watch-cats in Oriental temples centuries before. They had hidden in the shadows. They had crouched on high walls, ready to spring on any intruder to tear his face to ribbons.

The figure in the window advanced secretly toward the hall. Phut Phat experienced a sense of the familiar. It was the man with the shiny silver stick. This time, though, his presence seemed sinister. A small blue light now glowed from the head of the cane. And instead of leaning on it, the man pointed it ahead to guide his way out of the library and toward the staircase. As the intruder passed the dresser, Phut Phat's fur rose. Something told him, "Spring at him!" But vague fears held him back.

The man moved downstairs, unaware of two glowing diamond eyes that watched him in the blackness. Soon Phut Phat heard noises in the dining room. He sensed evil. Safe on top of the dresser, he trembled.

When the man reappeared, he was carrying a bulky load, which he took to the library window. Now the man appeared again, following a pool of blue light. As he approached the dresser, Phut Phat shifted his feet.

"Get him!" commanded a savage impulse within him.

"Stay!" warned the fear throbbing in his head.

"Get him! . . . Now . . . now . . . NOW!"

Phut Phat sprang at the man's head, ripping with razor claws wherever they sank into flesh.

The hideous scream that came from the intruder was like

an electric shock. It sent Phut Phat sailing through space—up the stairs—into the bedroom—under the bed.

For a long time he shook uncontrollably. His mouth was parched, and his ears inside-out with horror at what had happened. He huddled in the darkness. Blood soiled his claws. Slowly he licked them clean. Then he tucked his paws under his warm body and waited.

When One and Two came home, he sensed their arrival even before the taxicab door slammed. He should have bounded to meet them. But the experience had left him in a daze, weak and unsure. He heard the rattle of the front door lock. He heard feet climbing the stairs, and the click of the light switch in the room where he waited in bewilderment under the bed.

"John!" shrieked One. "Someone's been in this room. We've been robbed!"

"What! How do you know?"

"My jewel case. Look! It's open—and empty!"

Two threw open a closet door. "Your furs are still here, Helen. What about money? Did you have any money in the house?"

"I never leave money around. But the silver? What about the silver? John, go and see. I'm afraid to look . . . No! Wait a minute!" One's voice rose in panic. "Where's Phut Phat? What's happened to Phut Phat?"

"I don't know," said Two with alarm. "I haven't seen him since we came in."

They searched the house, calling his name—unaware, with their limited senses, that Phut Phat was right there under the bed.

At last, crawling on their hands and knees, they spied two eyes glowing red under the bed. They drew him out gently. One hugged him and rubbed her face, wet and salty, on his fur. Two stood by, stroking him with a heavy hand. Comforted and reassured, Phut Phat stopped trembling.

One continued to hold Phut Phat in her arms. He didn't even jump down after two strange men were admitted to the house. They asked questions and examined all the rooms.

"Everything is insured," One told them. "But the silver cannot be replaced. It's old and very rare. Is there any chance of getting it back, Lieutenant?" She fingered Phut Phat's ears nervously.

"At this point it's hard to say," the detective said. "But you may be able to help us. Have you noticed any strange incidents lately? Any unusual telephone calls?"

"Yes," said One. "Several times recently the phone has rung. When we answered it, there was no one on the line."

"That's the usual method. They wait until they know you're not at home."

One gazed into Phut Phat's eyes. "Did the phone ring tonight while we were out, Phuffy?" she asked, shaking him lovingly. "If only Phut Phat could tell us what happened! He must have had a terrifying experience. Thank heaven he wasn't harmed."

Phut Phat raised his paw.

"If only Phuffy could tell us who was here."

Phut Phat paused. He stared at One's forehead.

"Have you folks noticed any strangers in the neighborhood?" the lieutenant was asking. "Anyone who would arouse suspicion?"

Phut Phat's body tensed. His blue eyes, brimming with knowledge, bored into that spot above One's eyebrows.

"No, I can't think of anyone," she said. "Can you, John?"

Two shook his head.

"Poor Phuffy," said One. "See how he stares at me! He must be hungry. Does Phuffy want a little snack?"

Phut Phat squirmed.

"About those bloodstains on the windowsill," said the detective. "Would the cat attack an intruder viciously enough to draw blood?"

"Heavens, no!" said One. "He's just a pampered little house pet. We found him hiding under the bed, scared stiff."

"And you're sure you can't remember any unusual incidents lately? Has anyone come to the house who might have seen the silver or jewelry? Repairman? Window washer?"

"I wish I could be more helpful," said One. "But honestly, I can't think of a single suspect."

Phut Phat gave up.

Wriggling free, he jumped down from One's lap and walked toward the door with his head down in disgust. He knew! It was the man with the stick. But it was useless to try to communicate. The human mind was closed so tight that nothing important could ever penetrate. And One was so busy with her own chatter that her mind . . .

The jiggle of keys caught Phut Phat's attention. He turned and saw Two swinging his key chain back and forth, back and forth, saying nothing. Two always did more thinking than talking. Perhaps Phut Phat had been trying to communicate with the wrong mind.

Now it's time for YOU to be The Reader as Detective.

What do you think Phut Phat did?
Read on to see if you are right!

Phut Phat froze in his position of concentration. The key chain swung back and forth. Phut Phat fastened his blue eyes on three wrinkles just underneath Two's hairline. Phut Phat concentrated. The key chain swung back and forth, back and forth. Phut Phat kept *concentrating*.

"Wait a minute," said Two, coming out of his puzzled silence. "I just thought of something. Helen, remember that party we gave a couple of weeks ago. There was one guest we couldn't account for. A man with a silver cane."

"Why, yes! The man who was so curious about the cage on the fire escape. Why didn't I think of him. Lieutenant, he was terribly interested in our Georgian silver."

Two said, "Does that suggest anything to you, Lieutenant?"

"Yes, it does." The detective exchanged nods with his partner.

"This man," One volunteered, "had a very soft voice and a charming manner."

"We know him," the detective said grimly. "We know his method. What you tell us fits perfectly. But we didn't know that he was operating in this neighborhood again."

One said, "What mystifies me is the blood on the window-sill."

Phut Phat arched his body in a long, luxurious stretch. He walked from the room, looking for a soft, dark, quiet place. Now he would sleep. He felt relaxed and satisfied. He had made vital contact with a human mind, so perhaps—after all—there was hope. Some day they might learn the system. They might learn to open their minds and receive. They still had a long way to go—but there was hope.

I. The Reader as Detective

Read each question below. Then write the letter of the correct answer to each question. Remember, the symbol next to each question identifies the *kind* of reading skill that particular question helps you to develop.

1. Suppose this story appeared as a news article in a newspaper. Which of the following would make the best headline?

   a. Phut Phat Feels Fine Following Fight
   b. Concentrating Cat Catches Crook
   c. Gracious Guest Takes Treasures

2. One and Two discovered that the burglar
   a. attacked Phut Phat.
   b. stole some money.
   c. took the silver.

3. Phut Phat thought that human beings
   a. were smarter than cats.
   b. were not as smart as cats.
   c. knew how to speak to cats properly.

4. Which happened last?
   a. One and Two went to see the Burmese kittens.
   b. A detective asked One and Two questions.
   c. Phut Phat sprang at the man's head.

5. We may infer that the guest asked to inspect Phut Phat's cage on the fire escape because he

  a. was curious to see what the cage looked like.
  b. wanted to buy a similar cage for his cat.
  c. was looking for a way to break in.

6. Phut Phat watched "petrified" as the burglar opened the library window. Which expression best defines the word *petrified?*

  a. in the manner of a pet
  b. filled with joy and delight
  c. turned to stone

7. Which statement expresses an opinion?

  a. The charming guest leaned heavily on a shiny cane.
  b. Phut Phat was a Siamese cat.
  c. Cats make better pets than dogs.

8. When the police find the burglar, they will probably discover that

  a. he has scratches on his head.
  b. he has decided to "go straight."
  c. it was the first crime he ever committed.

9. After the burglar left, Phut Phat shook uncontrollably and his "mouth was parched." What is the meaning of the word *parched?*

  a. full   b. wet   c. dry

10. This story suggests that cats

  a. have a sixth sense.
  b. do not remember things well.
  c. should not be left home alone.

II. On the Trail of Story Elements

The **climax** of a story is the *turning point*. Usually, it is an event in the plot which determines how the story will end. Answer the questions below. Questions 11 and 12 refer to the climax of the story. Questions 13–15 review setting and characterization.

11. The climax of "Phut Phat Concentrates" occurs when

a. Phut Phat finally manages to communicate with Two.
b. Phut Phat is placed in his wire cage on the fire escape.
c. the uninvited guest calls Phut Phat a champion.

12. What happens as a result of the climax?

a. One and Two learned how to communicate with cats.
b. The detectives learned who the robber was.
c. Phut Phat was given a special treat.

13. What is the setting of the story?

a. a small cottage
b. a large apartment house
c. a comfortable three-story brick house

14. "Phut Phat Concentrates" takes place in

a. a small village.
b. a city.
c. the country.

15. This story may be considered unusual because the main character is

a. a house robber.
b. a cat.
c. a couple called One and Two.

III. Finding Word Meanings

Now it's time to be a word detective. Below are ten words which appear in "Phut Phat Concentrates." Study the words and the definitions beside them. Then complete the following paragraphs by using each word only *once*.

		page
inferior	lower in quality; below the average	98
acknowledgment	the act of admitting that something is true; agreement	100

page

sculpture	a figure carved or made out of stone, wood, clay, etc.	100
dignified	self-respecting and proud; stately	100
strictly	very carefully; absolutely	100
attractive	pleasing	100
pampered	allowed too many privileges	105
penetrate	to make a way through; pierce	106
arched	curved	107
mystifies	bewilders; puzzles	107

Among animal lovers there is agreement, or __16__, that cats make excellent pets. To begin with, cats are intelligent. With their piercing eyes, they seem to be able to __17__ life's deepest mysteries. Cats are also unusually clean. They always wash themselves carefully after eating. This is a routine which they always follow __18__.

Most people enjoy the stately, or __19__, manner with which cats conduct themselves. Indeed, cats seem to suggest that non-cats are less worthy and are therefore __20__.

Few animals are as graceful as a cat. When a cat sits silently, its back highly __21__, it resembles a fine object of __22__.

It is not surprising, therefore, that cats are sometimes __23__ by their owners. This special attention sometimes puzzles or __24__ people who do not find cats so pleasing, or __25__.

IV. Telling About the Case

A. Suppose Phut Phat were capable of speaking. What do you think he would tell the detectives? Include as many details as possible in your answer. You may find it helpful to make a list or outline in preparing your answer.

B. Explain why this story is titled "Phut Phat Concentrates." Think of another appropriate name for the story. Later, you and your classmates may have an opportunity to share titles and select the favorite ones.

The Disappearing Man

by Isaac Asimov

I'm not often on the spot when Dad's on one of his cases,
but I couldn't help it this time.

I was coming home from the library that afternoon, when
a man dashed by me and ran full speed into an alley between
two buildings. It was rather late, and I figured the best thing
to do was to keep on moving toward home. Dad says a nosy
fourteen-year-old isn't likely to make it to fifteen.

But in less than a minute, two policemen came running. I
didn't wait for them to ask. "He went in there," I said.

One of them rushed in, came out, and shouted, "There's a
door open. He went inside. Go 'round to the front."

They must have given the alarm, because in a few minutes, three police cars drove up, there were plainclothesmen
on the scene, and the building was surrounded.

I knew I shouldn't be hanging around. Innocent bystand-
ers get in the way of the police. Just the same, I was there
when it started and, from what I heard the police saying, I
knew they were after this man, Stockton. He was a loner
who'd pulled off some pretty spectacular jewel robberies over
the last few months. I knew about it because Dad is a detective on the force, and he was on the case.

"Slippery fellow," he said, "but when you work alone,
there's no one to double-cross you."

111

I said, "Doesn't he have to work with someone, Dad? He's got to have a fence—someone to peddle the jewels."

"If he has," said Dad, "we haven't located him. And why don't you get on with your homework?" (He always says that when he thinks I'm getting too interested in his cases.)

Well, they had him now. Some jeweler must have pushed the alarm button.

The alley he ran into was closed on all sides but the street, and he hadn't come out. There was a door there that was open, and he must have gone in. The police had the possible exits guarded. They even had a couple of men on the roof.

I was just beginning to wonder if Dad would be involved, when another car came up and he got out. First thing he saw me and stopped dead. "Larry! What are you doing here?"

"I was on the spot, Dad. Stockton ran past me into the alley."

"Well, get out of here. There's liable to be shooting."

I backed away, but I didn't back off all the way. Once my father went into the building, I got into his car. The driver knew me, and he said, "You better go home, Larry. I'm going to have to help with the search, so I can't stay here to keep an eye on you."

"Sure, you go on," I said. "I'll be leaving in a minute." But I didn't. I wanted to do some thinking first.

Nobody leaves doors open in New York City. If that door into the alley was open, Stockton must have opened it. That meant he had to have a key; there wasn't time to pick the lock. That must mean he worked out of that building.

I looked at the building. It was an old one, four stories high. It had small businesses in it, and you could still see the painted signs in the windows in the fading light.

On the second-floor window, it said, "Klein and Levy, Tailors." Above that was a theatrical costumer, and on the top floor was a jeweler's. That jeweler's made sense out of it.

If Stockton had a key to the building, he probably worked with that jeweler. Dad would figure all that out.

I waited for the sound of shots, pretty scared Dad might get hurt. But nothing happened. Maybe Stockton would see he was cornered and just give in. I hoped so. At least they

didn't have to evacuate the building. Late on Saturday, I supposed it would be deserted.

After a while, I got tired of waiting. I chose a moment
when no policemen were looking and moved quickly to the
building entrance. Dad would be hopping mad when he saw
me, but I was curious. I figured they had Stockton, and I
wanted to see him.

They didn't have him.

There was a fat man in a vest in the lobby. He looked
scared, and I guess he was the watchman. He kept saying, "I
didn't see *any*body."

Policemen were coming down the stairs and out of the old
elevator, all shaking their heads.

My father was pretty angry. He said, "No one has anything?"

A police sergeant said, "Donovan said no one got out on
the roof. All the doors and windows are covered."

"If he didn't get out," said my father, in a low voice that
carried, "then he's in the building."

"We can't find him," said the sergeant. "He's nowhere inside."

My father said, "It isn't a big building—"

"We had the watchman's keys. We've looked everywhere."

"Then how do we know he went into the building in the
first place? Who saw him go in?"

There was a silence. A lot of policemen were milling about
the lobby now, but no one said anything. So I spoke up. "I
did, Dad."

Dad whirled and looked at me and made a funny sound in
the back of his throat that meant I was in for it for still being
there. "You said you saw him run into the alley," he said.
"That's not the same thing."

"He didn't come out, Dad. There was no place else for him
to go."

"But you didn't actually see him go in, did you?"

"He couldn't go up the side of the buildings. There
wouldn't have been time for him to reach the roof before the
police—"

But Dad wasn't listening. "Did *anyone* actually see him go in?"

Of course no one said anything, and I could see my father was going to call the whole thing off, and then when he got me home I was going to get the talking-to of my life.

The thought of that talking-to must have stimulated my brain, I guess. I looked about the lobby desperately, and said, "But, Dad, he *did* go into the building, and he didn't disappear. There he is right now. That man there." I pointed and then I dropped down and rolled out of the way.

There wasn't any shooting. The man I pointed to was close to the door—he must have been edging toward it—and now he made a dash for it. He almost made it, but a policeman who had been knocked down grabbed his leg and then everyone piled on him. Later they had the jeweler, too.

I went home after Stockton was caught, and when my father got home much later, he did have some things to say about my risking my life. But he also said, "You got onto that theatrical costume bit very nicely, Larry."

I said, "Well, I was sure he went into the building and was familiar with it. He could get into the costumer's if he had to, and they would be bound to have policemen's uniforms. I figured if he could dump his jacket and pants and get into a policeman's uniform quickly, he could just walk out of the building."

Dad said, "You're right. Even after he got outside, he could pretend he was dealing with the crowd and then just walk away."

Mom said, "But how did you know which policeman it was, Larry? Don't tell me you know every policeman by sight."

Now it's time for YOU to be The Reader as Detective.

How was Larry able to identify Stockton?
Read on to see if you are right!

"I didn't have to Mom," I said. "I figured if he got a policeman's uniform at the costumer's, he had to work fast and grab any one he saw. And they wouldn't have much of an assortment of sizes anyway. So I just looked around for a policeman whose uniform didn't fit, and when I saw one with trouser legs stopping above his ankles, I knew he was Stockton."

I. The Reader as Detective

Read each question below. Then write the letter of the correct answer to each question. Remember, the symbol next to each question identifies the *kind* of reading skill that particular question helps you to develop.

1. This story tells mainly about

   a. how the police surrounded a building.
   b. how a young man helped capture a criminal.
   c. how Stockton stole some jewelry.

2. Larry's father was a

   a. jeweler.
   b. watchman.
   c. detective.

3. Which one of the following was true of Stockton?

   a. He was a thief who usually worked with a gang.
   b. He was wearing a uniform which was too short.
   c. He had never been in the building before.

4. Several policemen were "milling about the lobby." As used in this sentence, what is the meaning of the word *milling?*

   a. grinding grain into flour
   b. moving around
   c. running a mile

5. How old was Larry?

   a. fourteen years old
   b. fifteen years old
   c. sixteen years old

6. Stockton was in a building which was

   a. about ten stories high.
   b. four stories tall and old.
   c. new and filled with large businesses.

7. Which one of the following statements does *not* express an opinion?

   a. There is no job more risky than that of a police officer.
   b. Larry's father spoke to Larry about his risking his life.
   c. Some day Larry will probably get hurt by risking his life.

8. The story is called "The Disappearing Man" because

   a. Larry thought that he had better disappear before his father arrived.
   b. Larry couldn't see the burglar's face clearly.
   c. no one could find the thief.

9. When did Larry explain how he knew which policeman was Stockton?

   a. as soon as Larry met his father
   b. when Stockton came out of the building
   c. after Larry went home

10. We may infer that if Larry hadn't been present, Stockton would have

   a. shot a policeman.
   b. escaped.
   c. given himself up.

II. On the Trail of Story Elements

Answer the questions below. They will help you review the following story elements: setting, characterization, and plot.

11. The setting of the story is

   a. a building.   *b.* an alley.   *c.* a police station.

12. Where does the story take place?

    a. California   *c.* This information is not given.
    b. New York City

13. The main character in ''The Disappearing Man'' is

    a. Larry.   *c.* Stockton.
    b. Larry's father.

14. Which event occurred last in the plot of the story?

    a. Larry's dad pulled up in a car.
    b. A policeman grabbed Stockton by the leg.
    c. Larry saw a man dash into the alley.

15. Which one of the following facts plays the *most important* part in the plot of the story?

    a. the fact that the building would be deserted on Saturday
    b. the fact that there were painted signs in the windows of the building
    c. the fact that there was a theatrical costumer in the building

III. Finding Word Meanings

Now it's time to be a word detective. Listed below are five vocabulary words which appear in ''The Disappearing Man'' and five *new* vocabulary words for you to learn. Study the words and their definitions. Then complete the following paragraphs by using each vocabulary word only *once*.

		page
spectacular	sensational; highly interesting	111
evacuate	to empty	114
vest	a short, sleeveless garment which buttons in front	114
stimulated	roused or moved to action	115
assortment	variety; collection	116
skyscraper	a very tall building	
faulty	incorrect; poorly made or done	
douse	to throw water on	
fumes	vapors of smoke or gas	
injured	hurt	

Last week, there was a raging, __16__ fire in a very tall __17__ on Warren Street. The fire fighters began to __18__ the area with water, and quickly managed to __19__ everyone from the building. No one was seriously __20__, although a few people became ill from the __21__ from the blaze.

On TV, an official who was wearing a dark blue __22__ made an announcement. He stated that the fire had been caused by __23__ electrical wiring. He also said that the accident had roused, or __24__, the city to think about new ways to prevent fires. A wide __25__ of measures is being planned.

IV. Telling About the Case

A. Larry saw Stockton dash into an alley between two buildings. Explain why Larry thought that Stockton had a key to the building. If you wish look back to the story.
B. In the windows of the building, Larry saw painted signs for three small businesses. What were the businesses?
C. Which *one* of the businesses did Larry believe was Stockton's "fence"? Explain Larry's reasoning.

Geraldine Moore the Poet

by Toni Cade Bambara

Geraldine paused at the corner to pull up her knee
socks. The rubber bands she was using to hold them
up made her legs itch. She dropped her books on the sidewalk
while she gave a good scratch. But when she pulled the socks
up again, two fingers poked right through the top of her left
one.

"That stupid dog," she muttered to herself, grabbing her
books and crossing against traffic. "First he chews up my gym
suit and gets me into trouble, and now my socks."

Geraldine shifted her books to the other hand and kept
muttering angrily to herself about Mrs. Watson's dog, which
she minded two days a week for a dollar. She passed the hot-
dog man on the corner and waved. He shrugged as if to say
business was very bad.

Must be, she thought to herself. *Three guys before you had
to pack up and forget it. Nobody's got hot-dog money around
here.*

Geraldine turned down her street, wondering what her
sister Anita would have for her lunch. She was glad she didn't
have to eat the free lunches in high school any more. She was
sick of the funny-looking tomato soup and the dried-out
cheese sandwiches and those oranges that were more green
than orange.

120

When Geraldine's mother first took sick and went away, Geraldine had been on her own except when Miss Gladys next door came in on Thursdays and cleaned the apartment and made a meat loaf so Geraldine could have dinner. But in those days Geraldine never quite managed to get breakfast for herself. So she'd sit though social studies class, scraping her feet to cover up the noise of her stomach growling.

Now Anita, Geraldine's older sister, was living at home waiting for her husband to get out of the Army. She usually had something good for lunch—chicken and dumplings if she managed to get up in time, or baked ham from the night before and sweet-potato bread. But even if there was only a hot dog and some baked beans—sometimes just a TV dinner if those soap operas kept Anita glued to the TV set—anything was better than the noisy school lunchroom where monitors kept pushing you into a straight line or rushing you to the tables. Anything was better than that.

Geraldine was almost home when she stopped dead. Right outside her building was a pile of furniture and some boxes. That wasn't anything new. She had seen people get put out in the street before, but this time the ironing board looked familiar. And she recognized the big, ugly sofa standing on its arm, its underbelly showing the hole where Mrs. Watson's dog had gotten to it.

Miss Gladys was sitting on the stoop, and she looked up and took off her glasses. "Well, Gerry," she said slowly, wiping her glasses on the hem of her dress, "looks like you'll be staying with me for a while." She looked at the men carrying out a big box with an old doll sticking up over the edge. "Anita's upstairs. Go on up and get your lunch."

Geraldine stepped past the old woman and almost bumped into the superintendent. He took off his cap to wipe away the sweat.

"Darn shame," he said to no one in particular. "Poor people sure got a hard row to hoe."

"That's the truth," said Miss Gladys, standing up with her hands on her hips to watch the men set things on the sidewalk.

Upstairs, Geraldine went into the apartment and found Anita in the kitchen.

"I dunno, Gerry," Anita said, "I just don't know what we're going to do. But everything's going to be all right soon as Ma gets well." Anita's voice cracked as she set a bowl of soup before Geraldine.

"What's this?" Geraldine said.

"It's tomato soup, Gerry."

Geraldine was about to say something. But when she looked up at her big sister, she saw how Anita's face was getting all twisted as she began to cry.

That afternoon, Mr. Stern, the geometry teacher, started drawing cubes and cylinders on the board. Geraldine sat at her desk adding up a column of figures in her notebook—the rent, the light and gas bills, a new gym suit, some socks. Maybe they would move somewhere else, and she could have her own room. Geraldine turned the squares and triangles into little houses in the country.

"For your homework," Mr. Stern was saying with his back to the class, "set up your problems this way." He wrote GIVEN: in large letters, and then gave the formula for the first problem. Then he wrote TO FIND: and listed three items they were to include in their answers.

Geraldine started to raise her hand to ask what all these squares and angles had to do with solving real problems, like the ones she had. *Better not*, she warned herself, and sat on her hands. *Your big mouth got you in trouble last term.*

In hygiene class, Mrs. Potter kept saying that the body was a wonderful machine. Every time Geraldine looked up from her notebook, she would hear the same thing. "Right now your body is manufacturing all the proteins and tissues and energy you will need to get through tomorrow."

And Geraldine kept wondering, *How? How does my body know what it will need, when I don't even know what I'll need to get through tomorrow?*

As she headed down the hall to her next class, Geraldine remembered that she hadn't done the homework for English. Mrs. Scott had said to write a poem, and Geraldine had meant to do it at lunchtime. Afer all, there was nothing to it—a flower here, a raindrop there, moon, June, rose, nose. But the men carrying off the furniture had made her forget.

"And now put away your books," Mrs. Scott was saying as Geraldine tried to scribble a poem quickly. "Today we can give King Arthur's knights a rest. Let's talk about poetry."

Mrs. Scott moved up and down the aisles, talking about her favorite poems and reciting a line now and then. She got very excited whenever she passed a desk and could pick up the homework from a student who had remembered to do the assignment.

"A poem is your own special way of saying what you feel and what you see," Mrs. Scott went on, her lips moist. It was her favorite subject.

"Some poets write about the light that . . . that . . . makes the world sunny," she said, passing Geraldine's desk. "Sometimes an idea takes the form of a picture—an image."

For almost half an hour, Mrs. Scott stood at the front of the room, reading poems and talking about the lives of the great poets. Geraldine drew more houses, and designs for curtains.

"So for those who haven't done their homework, try it now," Mrs. Scott said. "Try expressing what it is like to be . . . to be alive in this . . . this glorious world."

"Oh, brother," Geraldine muttered to herself as Mrs. Scott moved up and down the aisles again, waving her hands and leaning over the students' shoulders and saying, "That's nice," or "Keep trying." Finally she came to Geraldine's desk and stopped, looking down at her.

"I can't write a poem," Geraldine said flatly, before she even realized she was going to speak at all. She said it very loudly, and the whole class looked up.

"And why not?" Mrs. Scott asked, looking hurt.

"I can't write a poem, Mrs. Scott, because nothing lovely's been happening in my life. I haven't seen a flower since Mother's Day, and the sun don't even shine on my side of the street. No robins come sing on my window sill."

Geraldine swallowed hard. She thought about saying that her father doesn't even come to visit any more, but changed her mind. "Just the rain comes," she went on, "and the bills come, and the men to move out our furniture. I'm sorry, but I can't write no pretty poem."

Teddy Johnson leaned over and was about to giggle and crack the whole class up, but Mrs. Scott looked so serious that he changed his mind.

> Now it's time for YOU to be The Reader as Detective.
>
> Why do you think Mrs. Scott looked so serious— and what do you think she said and *did?*
> Read on to see if you are right!

"You have just said the most . . . the most poetic thing, Geraldine Moore," said Mrs. Scott. Her hands flew up to touch the silk scarf around her neck. " 'Nothing lovely's been happening in my life.' " She repeated it so quietly that everyone had to lean forward to hear.

"Class," Mrs. Scott said very sadly, clearing her throat, "you have just heard the best poem you will ever hear." She went to the board and stood there for a long time staring at the chalk in her hand.

"I'd like you to copy it down," she said. She wrote it just as Geraldine had said it, bad grammar and all.

Nothing lovely's been happening in my life.
I haven't seen a flower since Mother's Day,
And the sun don't even shine on my side of the street.
No robins come sing on my window sill.
Just the rain comes, and the bills come,
And the men to move out our furniture.
I'm sorry, but I can't write no pretty poem.

Mrs. Scott stopped writing, but she kept her back to the class for a long time—long after Geraldine had closed her notebook.

And even when the bell rang, and everyone came over to smile at Geraldine or to tap her on the shoulder or to kid her about being the school poet, Geraldine waited for Mrs. Scott to put the chalk down and turn around. Finally Geraldine stacked up her books and started to leave. Then she thought she heard a whimper—the way Mrs. Watson's dog whimpered sometimes—and she saw Mrs. Scott's shoulders shake a little.

I. The Reader as Detective

Read each question below. Then write the letter of the correct answer to each question. Remember, the symbol next to each question identifies the *kind* of reading skill that particular question helps you to develop.

1. After Geraldine's mother became ill, Geraldine
   a. went to live with some friends.
   b. lived alone for a while.
   c. moved in with Miss Gladys, a neighbor.

2. Mrs. Scott's favorite subject was
   a. grammar.   c. poetry.
   b. spelling.

3. How do you think Geraldine felt when she saw the familiar, old sofa in the street?

a. curious but pleased   c. sad and troubled
b. satisfied and content

4. Geraldine heard "a whimper" and saw Mrs. Scott's shoulders shake a little. Which expression best defines the word *whimper*?

a. low, sobbing sound   c. sweet song
b. loud, crashing noise

5. Geraldine stated that

a. it was fun to be alive in this glorious world.
b. the sun often shone on her side of the street.
c. nothing lovely had been happening in her life.

6. Probably, Mrs. Scott "kept her back to the class for a long time" because

a. she didn't want the class to see that she was very upset.
b. she was trying to hide the fact that she was angry.
c. she was attempting to memorize Geraldine's poem.

7. Which happened last?

a. Mrs. Scott stood for a long time staring at the chalk in her hand.
b. Geraldine passed the hot-dog man and waved.
c. Mr. Stern drew cubes and cylinders on the board.

8. Which one of the following statements expresses an opinion?

a. Geraldine remembered that she hadn't done the homework for English.
b. Everyone knows that mathematics is the most important subject.
c. Anita's voice cracked as she began to cry.

9. The last paragraph of the story suggests that Mrs. Scott was

a. thinking about her next class.
b. filled with emotion by what Geraldine had said.
c. not a good teacher.

10. This story is mainly about how Geraldine

   a. managed to pass her English class.

   b. added up a column of figures during math.

   c. created a poem out of her powerful feelings.

II. On the Trail of Story Elements

"Geraldine Moore the Poet" presents two unforgettable characters—Geraldine and Mrs. Scott. Answer the following questions. They will help you review characterization in a short story.

11. Which statement best characterizes Geraldine?

   a. She had fine clothes and plenty of money.

   b. Although she was not rich, she enjoyed many comforts and luxuries.

   c. She was poor and lived a hard life.

12. There is evidence in the story that Geraldine

   a. liked all of her subjects in school.

   b. sometimes got into trouble in school by speaking up.

   c. was not able to take care of herself.

13. Which sentence from the story gives a clue to Geraldine's hopes for the future?

   a. Geraldine turned the squares and triangles into little houses in the country.

   b. Geraldine turned down her street, wondering what her sister Anita would have for her lunch.

   c. Geraldine stepped past the old woman and almost bumped into the superintendent.

14. Mrs. Scott believed that poetry

   a. must always rhyme.

   b. is a person's special way of expressing what that person sees and feels.

   c. can be written only by great poets and writers.

15. Through her actions, Mrs. Scott demonstrated that she

   a. cared very deeply about her students.

   b. was not very interested in her students.

   c. thought that poetry belonged in books, not in real life.

III. Finding Word Meanings

Now it's time to be a word detective. Listed below are five vocabulary words which appear in "Geraldine Moore the Poet" and five *new* vocabulary words for you to learn. Study the words and their definitions. Then complete the following paragraphs by using each word only *once*.

		page
geometry	a branch of mathematics which deals with circles, squares, cubes, triangles, etc.	122
formula	a rule or method for doing something	122
reciting	saying part of a lesson; answering questions in class	123
assignment	a piece of work to be done	123
image	a picture in the mind	123
confidential	secret or private	
competent	able; capable	
speculate	to think carefully about; consider	
merit	value or worth	
conscientiously	carefully; done with great care	

Winston was a very capable, or __16__, student who had always done well in school. Suddenly, however, he began to have trouble in his __17__ class. He did each piece of work, or __18__, carefully and __19__. Still, he couldn't seem to grasp the subject.

After class one day, his teacher, Mrs. Weng, had a private and __20__ talk with Winston. "Let me consider, or __21__ about your problem," said Mrs. Weng. "I think it likely that your difficulty lies in how you *approach* the work. Here is a suggestion which I think has __22__. Try to see each problem as a very interesting game or puzzle. If you keep this picture, or __23__, in mind, I think you'll improve."

That proved to be Winston's special method, or __24__, for success. Now he's doing well, and enjoys __25__ aloud in class.

IV. Telling About the Case

A. Mrs. Scott explained that some poets "write about the light that makes the world sunny." Was Geraldine this kind of poet? Explain.

B. Explain what you think Mrs. Scott meant when she told the class: "You have just heard the best poem you will ever hear." Why did Mrs. Scott say this very sadly?

C. Why did Mrs. Scott keep her back to the class for a long time—long after Geraldine had closed her notebook?

A Day's Wait

by Ernest Hemingway

He came into the room to shut the windows while we were still in bed, and I saw he looked ill. He was shivering, his face was white, and he walked slowly as though it ached to move.

"What's the matter, Schatz?"

"I've got a headache."

"You'd better go back to bed."

"No. I'm all right."

"You go to bed. I'll see you when I'm dressed."

But when I came downstairs he was dressed, sitting by the fire, looking a very sick and miserable boy of nine years. When I put my hand on his forehead I knew he had a fever.

"You go up to bed," I said. "You're sick."

"I'm all right," he said.

When the doctor came he took the boy's temperature.

"What is it?" I asked him.

"One hundred and two."

Downstairs, the doctor left three different medicines in different colored capsules with instructions for giving them. He seemed to know all about influenza and said there was nothing to worry about if the fever did not go above one hundred and four degrees. This was a light epidemic of flu, and there was no danger if you avoided pneumonia.

Back in the room I wrote the boy's temperature down and made note of the time to give the various capsules.

"Do you want me to read to you?"

130

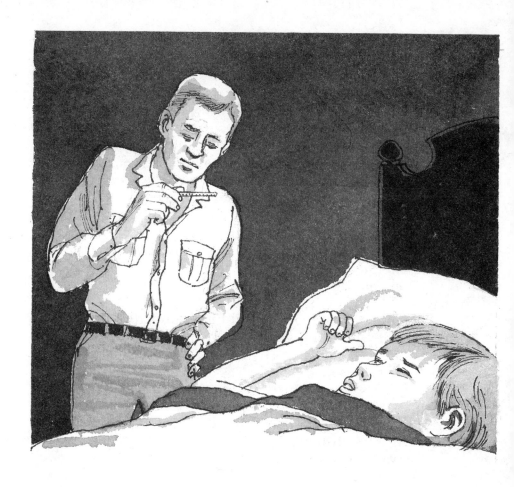

"All right. If you want to," said the boy. His face was very white, and there were dark areas under his eyes. He lay still in the bed and seemed very detached from what was going on.

I read aloud from Howard Pyle's *Book of Pirates*, but I could see he was not following what I was reading.

"How do you feel, Schatz?" I asked him.

"Just the same, so far," he said.

I sat at the foot of the bed and read to myself while I waited for it to be time to give another capsule. It would have been natural for him to go to sleep, but when I looked up he was looking at the foot of the bed, looking very strangely.

"Why don't you try to go to sleep? I'll wake you up for the medicine."

"I'd rather stay awake."

After a while he said to me, "You don't have to stay in here with me, Papa, if it bothers you."

"It doesn't bother me."

"No, I mean you don't have to stay if it's going to bother you."

I thought perhaps he was a little lightheaded, and after giving him the prescribed capsules at eleven o'clock I went out for a while. It was a bright, cold day, the ground covered with a sleet that had frozen so that it seemed as if all the bare trees, the bushes, the cut brush, and all the grass and the bare ground had been varnished with ice.

At the house they said the boy had refused to let anyone come into the room.

"You can't come in," he said. "You mustn't get what I have."

I went up to him and found him in exactly the same position I had left him, white-faced; but with the tops of his cheeks flushed by the fever, staring still, as he had stared, at the foot of the bed.

I took his temperature.

"What is it?"

"Something like a hundred," I said. It was one hundred and two and four-tenths.

"It was a hundred and two," he said.

"Who said so?"

"The doctor."

"Your temperature is all right," I said. "It's nothing to worry about."

"I don't worry," he said, "but I can't keep from thinking."

"Don't think," I said. "Just take it easy."

"I'm taking it easy," he said and looked straight ahead. He was evidently holding tight onto himself about something.

"Take this with water."

"Do you think it will do any good?"

"Of course it will."

I sat down and opened the *Pirate* book and commenced to read, but I could see he was not following; so I stopped.

"About what time do you think I'm going to die?" he asked.

"What?"

"About how long will it be before I die?"

"You aren't going to die. What's the matter with you?"

"Oh, yes I am. I heard him say a hundred and two."

"People don't die with a fever of one hundred and two. That's a silly way to talk."

"I know they do. At school in France the boys told me you can't live with forty-four degrees. I've got a hundred and two."

He had been waiting to die all day, ever since nine o'clock in the morning.

> Now it's time for YOU to be The Reader as Detective
>
> What do you think Schatz's father answered?
> Read on to see if you are right!

"You poor Schatz," I said. "Poor old Schatz. It's like miles and kilometers. You aren't going to die. That's a different thermometer. On that thermometer thirty-seven is normal. On this kind it's between ninety-eight and ninety-nine."

"Are you sure?"

"Absolutely," I said. "It's like miles and kilometers. You know, like how many kilometers we make when we do seventy miles in the car?"

"Oh," he said.

But his gaze at the foot of the bed relaxed slowly. The hold over himself relaxed too, finally, and the next day it was very slack, and he cried very easily at little things that were of no importance.

I. The Reader as Detective

Read each question below. Then write the letter of the correct answer to each question. Remember, the symbol next to each question identifies the *kind* of reading skill that particular question helps you to develop.

1. This story is mainly about

    a. different kinds of thermometers.

    b. how to fight the flu.

    c. how a boy faced death.

2. Schatz didn't want to let anyone come into the room because

    a. he was too tired to talk to anyone.

    b. he didn't want anyone to catch what he had.

    c. he was embarrassed that the room was messy.

3. Schatz's father gave him "the prescribed capsules" at eleven o'clock. What is the meaning of the word *prescribed?*

    a. expensive

    b. recommended

    c. dangerous

4. Probably, Schatz asked if the medicine would do any good because

    a. he had heard that the medicine was not effective.

    b. medicine didn't usually help him.

    c. he thought that his temperature was so high that medicine couldn't help him.

5. Which one of the following statements expresses an opinion?

    a. Papa read aloud from *Book of Pirates.*

    b. Schatz's face was white, but his cheeks were flushed.

    c. There is nothing as annoying as a summer cold.

6. The boy in bed was very still and seemed "detached from what was going on." Which expression best defines the word *detached?*

    a. separated or removed

    b. interested or concerned

    c. lively or active

7. Which happened first?

   a. Papa gave the boy the capsules and went out for a while.

   b. The doctor left instructions for giving the medicine.

   c. Schatz said it was not possible to live with a temperature of forty-four degrees.

8. What did the doctor do?

   a. He took the boy's temperature.

   b. He left three different medicines.

   c. Both of the above.

9. The frozen sleet made it seem as if the ground "had been varnished with ice." As used in this sentence, which expression best defines the word *varnished?*

   a. coated with a smooth and shining finish

   b. filled with large and heavy bumps

   c. broken into many sharp pieces

10. The last paragraph of the story suggests that Schatz

   a. had been controlling himself with great effort.

   b. had never even thought about dying.

   c. will be well in about two weeks.

II. On the Trail of Story Elements

Ernest Hemingway, the author of "A Day's Wait," is one of America's most famous authors. He is known for his style of writing, as well as for the tone he creates. Answer the following questions. They will help you review style and tone in a short story.

11. Judging by "A Day's Wait," which one of the following is true of Hemingway's style?

   a. There are many short passages of *dialogue*, or conversation.

   b. There are many long passages of description.

   c. Most of the sentences are long and difficult to understand.

12. One of the most striking things about the style of "A Day's Wait" is that

    a. much of the information given in the story is unnecessary.

    b. the paragraphs are very long.

    c. just about every sentence in the story is important.

13. Almost all of the action of the story takes place

    a. over a long period of time.

    b. in France.

    c. between two characters.

14. Which expression best describes the tone of the story?

    a. light and amusing

    b. powerful and moving

    c. humorous or comic

15. Select the sentence that best describes the author's attitude toward Schatz.

    a. He thought that Schatz was brave.

    b. He thought that Schatz was a coward.

    c. He had no sympathy at all for Schatz.

III. Finding Word Meanings

Now it's time to be a word detective. Listed below are five vocabulary words which appear in "A Day's Wait" and five *new* vocabulary words for you to learn. Study the words and their definitions. Then complete the following paragraphs by using each vocabulary word only *once*.

		page
influenza	a disease caused by a virus	130
epidemic	the rapid spread of a disease among many people in an area	130
flushed	made red in color	132
evidently	obviously	132
commenced	began; started	132
collapse	to fall down; cave in	
energetic	very active	

confirmed	proved to be true; established
acute	sharp and severe
symptoms	signs; signs related to a disease

Usually, Omara was lively, very active, and __16__. Suddenly, however, she felt so weak and she just wanted to __17__. Her face was hot and __18__, and she had very sharp, or __19__, pains in her arms and legs. All of this suggested that Omara was ill, __20__.

Omara wondered if she might have __21__. There was an __22__ in town; almost everyone she knew was sick.

Later, the doctor __23__ that Omara had the flu. She gave her some medicine and recommended rest. A few days afterward, Omara's __24__ were gone and she __25__ to feel like her old self again.

IV. Telling About the Case

A. Explain why the story is entitled "A Day's Wait." How does the title heighten the effect of the story?

B. Schatz refused to go to sleep. Instead, he looked strangely at the foot of the bed. Explain Schatz's actions.

C. The next day, Schatz cried very easily at little things that were of no importance. Why do you think he acted that way?

"The tiger sprang, launching himself as though his rear legs were
made of powerful steel springs. His left paw flashed . . ."

The Tiger's Heart

by Jim Kjelgaard

The approaching jungle night was a threat. As it grew
darker, silence came over the village. People were
silent. Cattle stood quietly. Chickens did not move and goats
made no noise. It had been that way for centuries and thus
would it continue to be. The inhabitants of the village knew
the jungle—knew its paths and rivers. They knew its deer and
crocodiles, its screaming green parrots and many other crea-
tures.

That was the daytime jungle they could see, feel and hear.
But at night everything became different. When darkness
came, the jungle was alive with strange and horrible things
which no man had ever seen and no man could describe. They
were shadows that had no substance. One was unaware of
them until they struck and killed. When morning came, they
changed themselves back into the shape of familiar things.
Because night was a time of the unknown, night had to be a
time of fear.

Except, thought Pepe Garcia, to the man who owned a rifle. As the night closed in, Pepe reached out to his rifle, to
make sure that it was close to him. As long as it was, he was
king.

That was only fair, for the rifle had cost him dearly. With
eleven others from his village, Pepe had gone to help chop a
clearing for the new road. They used machetes, the indispensable long knife that all jungle dwellers used. They had

worked hard. Unlike the rest, Pepe had saved every peso.*
With his savings, he had bought his rifle, a supply of powder,
and some bullets.

The rifle had cost him many pesos. But it was worth the
price. The jungle at night was fear itself. But no man with a
rifle had to fear. The others had only machetes with which to
guard themselves from the terrors that came in the darkness.
They were willing to pay well for protection. Pepe went
peacefully to sleep.

He did not know what awakened him, only that something
was near. He listened carefully, but there was no change in
the jungle's monotonous night sounds. Still, something was
not as it should be.

Then he heard it. At the far end of the village, near Juan
Aria's hut, a goat bleated uneasily. Silence followed. The goat
bleated again, louder and more fearful. There was a rush of
small hoofs, a frightened bleat cut short, then silence again.

Pepe correctly interpreted what he had heard. A tiger, a
jaguar, had come in the night. It had leaped over the fence
which surrounded the village, and had made off with one of
Juan Aria's goats.

Pepe went peacefully back to sleep. When morning came,
Juan Aria would certainly come to him.

Pepe did not awaken until the sun was up. Then he came
out of his hut, had breakfast, and awaited the visitor he expected.

Presently Pepe saw two men, Juan Aria and his brother.
They were coming up one of the village paths. Others stared
with curiosity, but nobody else came because their flocks had
not been raided. They had no wish to pay a hunter.

Pepe waited until the two were near. Then he said, "*Buenos dias.*" (Good day)

"*Buenos dias,*" they replied.

They sat down in the sun, looking at nothing in particular.
Finally, Juan Aria said, "I brought my goats into the village
last night. I thought they would be safe."

"And they were not?"

"They were not. Something came and killed one, a fine

*peso: a unit of money used in various countries of Latin America white and black nanny, my favorite. When the thing left, the goat went too. Never again shall I see her alive."

"What killed your goat?" Pepe inquired.

"This morning I saw the tracks of a tiger."

"Did you hear it approach?"

"I heard it."

"Then why did you not defend your flock?"

Juan Aria motioned with his hands. "To attack a tiger with nothing but a machete would be madness."

"That is true," Pepe agreed. "Let us hope that the next time it is hungry, this tiger will not come back for another goat."

"But it will!"

Pepe relaxed. For what Juan Aria had said greatly improved Pepe's bargaining position. And it was true that, having had a taste of easy game, the tiger would come again. Only death would end his attacks. And since he knew where to find Juan Aria's goats, he would continue to attack them.

Pepe said, "That is bad, for a man may lose many goats to a tiger."

"Unless a hunter kills him," Juan Aria said.

"Unless a hunter kills him," Pepe agreed.

"That is why I have come to you, Pepe," Juan Aria said. A troubled frown came over his face. "I hope you will follow and kill this tiger, for you are the only man who can do so."

"It would give me pleasure to kill him. But I cannot work for nothing."

"Nor do I expect you to. Even a tiger will not eat an entire goat, and you are sure to find what is left of my favorite nanny. Whatever the tiger has not eaten, you may have for your pay."

Pepe bristled and grew angry. "You are saying that I should put myself and my rifle to work for dead meat left by a tiger?"

"No, no!" Juan Aria said. "In addition I will give you one live goat!"

"Three goats."

"I am a poor man!" the other wailed. "You would bankrupt me!"

"No man with twenty-nine goats is poor," said Pepe,

"though he may be if a tiger raids his flock a sufficient number of times."

"I will give you one goat!"

"Two goats," said Pepe.

"You drive a hard bargain," Juan Aria said, "but I cannot deny you now. Kill the tiger."

Slowly, Pepe took his rifle from the fine blanket upon which it lay when he was not carrying it. Then he took his powder horn and bullet pouch. He strapped his machete on and made his way toward Juan Aria's hut. A half-dozen children followed.

"Begone!" Pepe ordered.

They fell behind, but continued to follow until Pepe came to the place where Juan Aria's goats had spent the night. He glanced at the dust, and saw the tiger's great paw marks imprinted there. It was a huge cat, lame in the right front paw. It might have been injured in a battle with another tiger.

Expertly, Pepe located the place where it had jumped back over the fence. The tiger had carried the sixty-pound goat in its jaws, but only a few branches were disturbed at the place where it had leaped.

Pepe did not look around, but he was aware of the villagers watching him. He knew that their glances would be full of respect. Most of the men went into the jungle to work with their machetes. But none would work where tigers were known to be. No one would dare to follow a tiger's trail. Only Pepe dared and, because he did, he must be honored and respected.

Pepe moved on. Behind him, he heard mingled sighs of relief and admiration. A raiding tiger was a real and terrible threat. Goats and cattle were not easily come by. The man with a rifle—the man able to protect them—must necessarily be a hero.

Once in the jungle, Pepe became as alert as a doe. A rifle might be a symbol of power. But unless a man was also a hunter, a rifle did him no good. Impressing the villagers was one thing. Hunting a tiger was another.

Pepe knew that tigers could move with incredible swiftness. They were strong enough to kill an ox, and they feared nothing.

To Pepe's trained eyes, there was a distinct trail. It consisted of an occasional drop of blood from the dead goat, a bent or broken plant, and paw prints in soft places.

Within the first quarter mile, Pepe knew many things about this tiger. He was not old, for his was not the slow gait of an old cat. And the ease with which he had leaped over the fence with a goat in his jaws was evidence of his strength.

Pepe stopped to load his rifle. Everything must be just right. When he saw the tiger, he must shoot straight and true. Warned by some jungle sense, Pepe slowed his pace. A moment later he found his game.

He came upon it suddenly in a grove of palm trees. Because he had not expected it there, Pepe did not see it until it was nearer than safety allowed.

The tiger crouched at the base of a tree. The beast's front paws were on what remained of the dead goat. It did not snarl or even twitch its tail. But there was a deadly quality about the big cat, and great tension. The tiger was bursting with raw anger that seemed to swell and grow.

Pepe stopped in his tracks. Cold fear crept up his spine. But he did not give way to fear. Carefully, he brought the rifle to his shoulder and took aim. He had only one bullet and there would be no time to reload. But even a tiger could not withstand the smash of a shot between his eyes. Pepe steadied the rifle.

His fingers tightened slowly on the trigger, for he must not let nervousness spoil his aim. When he pulled the trigger, Pepe's brain and body became numb.

There was no satisfying roar. There was no puff of black smoke coming from the muzzle. Instead there was only a sudden hiss, as though cold water had spilled on a hot stone. Pepe himself had loaded the rifle. But he could not have done it correctly.

Anger exploded in the tiger's deadly body. He snarled and got ready to charge. Lord of the jungle, he would crush this weak and miserable man who dared to interfere with him.

Pepe suddenly came back to reality. He leaned his rifle against a tree. In the same motion, he pulled out his machete.

It was now a hopeless fight. It would be decided in the tiger's favor, he knew, because not within the memory of the village's oldest inhabitant had any man ever killed a tiger with a machete. But he might as well fight hopelessly, as turn and run. For if he did that he would surely be killed. No tiger that attacked ever turned away.

Machete in hand, Pepe studied the onrushing cat. Pepe had read the tracks correctly, for the tiger's right front foot was swollen to almost twice the size of the other. It must have stepped on a poisonous thorn or been bitten by a snake.

Even with this handicap, a tiger was more than a match for a man armed only with a machete. But Pepe watched the right front paw carefully. If he had any advantage, it was there.

Then the tiger, a terrible engine of destruction, flung himself at Pepe. Pepe knew that the tiger's first strike would be exactly like this. He was ready for it. He swerved, bending his body outward as the great cat brushed past him. With all the strength in his powerful right arm, he swung the machete. He stopped his stroke just short of the tiger's back, for he knew, suddenly, that there was only one way to end this fight.

The tiger turned toward Pepe. Pepe held the machete in front of himself like a sword. He took a swift step backward. The tiger sprang, launching himself as though his rear legs were made of powerful steel springs. His left paw flashed at Pepe. It hooked in his shirt, ripping it as though it were paper. Burning claws sank into the flesh. Blood welled out.

Pepe did not try again to slash with the machete. Instead, he thrust, as he would have thrust with a knife or sword. The machete's point met the tiger's throat. Pepe put all his strength and weight behind it. The tiger gasped.

The tiger pulled himself away. But blood was rushing from his throat now and he shook his head, then stumbled and fell. He pulled himself erect, looked with dull eyes at Pepe, and dragged himself toward him. There was a low snarl. Then the tiger slumped to the ground. The tip of his tail twitched and was still.

Pepe stared. He hardly saw the blood that flowed from his wounded arm. He had done the impossible! He had killed a tiger with a machete! Pepe brushed a hand across his eyes. He trembled and took a step forward.

> Now it's time for YOU to be The Reader as Detective.
>
> What do you think Pepe is going to do?
> Read on to see if you are right!

He picked up his rifle and looked at it. There seemed to be nothing wrong with it. Then, with one foot against the tiger's head, he pulled the machete out.

He held the rifle close to the machete wound. Then he pulled the trigger. There was a puff of black smoke. All traces of the machete wound were gone. For a moment, Pepe felt regret. But he knew that this was the way it must be.

In his village, everybody had a machete. In his village, the man who owned a rifle was king.

I. The Reader as Detective

Read each question below. Then write the letter of the correct answer to each question. Remember, the symbol next to each question identifies the *kind* of reading skill that particular question helps you to develop.

1. The villagers respected Pepe because he
   a. taught the people of the village how to hunt.
   b. could protect them with his rifle.
   c. was the most intelligent person in the village.

2. By looking at the tiger's trail, Pepe could tell that the tiger
   a. was not very strong.
   b. was not very large.
   c. had an injured paw.

3. The tiger did not have "the slow gait of an old cat." Which expression best defines the word *gait*?

  a. manner of walking or running
  b. small, swinging fence
  c. expression around the eyes

4. What happened the first time that Pepe pulled the trigger?

  a. There was a loud roar.
  b. A puff of black smoke came from the muzzle.
  c. There was a sudden hiss.

5. Evidence in the story suggests that when he realized the tiger was dead, Pepe

  a. was filled with regret.
  b. was amazed.
  c. wondered if anyone had seen the fight.

6. Which one of the following statements from the story expresses an opinion?

  a. I brought my goats into the village last night.
  b. This morning I saw the tracks of a tiger.
  c. I hope you will follow and kill this tiger, for you are the only man who can do so.

7. Pepe saw the tiger's paw marks imprinted in the dust. As used in this sentence, what is the meaning of the word *imprinted*?

  a. glued   *b.* nailed   *c.* stamped

8. Which happened first?

  a. The tiger carried off one of Juan Aria's goats.
  b. Juan Aria and his brother came to speak to Pepe.
  c. The tiger flung himself at Pepe.

9. The last two paragraphs of the story suggest that Pepe

  a. wanted everyone to know that he killed the tiger with a machete.
  b. didn't want anyone to know that it was possible to kill a tiger with a machete.
  c. was thinking about selling his rifle to someone in the village.

10. This story is mainly about

    a. how Pepe obtained enough money to buy a rifle.

    b. how a man agreed to hunt down a tiger for two goats.

    c. how a hunter tracked down and killed a tiger.

II. On the Trail of Story Elements

Often, **conflict** is an important part of the plot of a short story. Conflict is the *clash*, the strong disagreement or struggle, between characters in a story. Sometimes, the conflict takes the form of a fight. Occasionally, characters struggle against nature, or have an inner, or *mental*, conflict with themselves.

Answer the following questions. They will help you review plot elements in a short story. Questions 11 and 12 refer to conflict.

11. The main conflict in "The Tiger's Heart" is between

    a. Juan Aria and Pepe Garcia.

    b. Pepe and the tiger.

    c. Pepe and the villagers.

12. The conflict in the story takes the form of

    a. a loud argument.

    b. a violent fight.

    c. a struggle using fists.

13. The climax of the story occurs when

    a. Pepe found the tiger's trail.

    b. Juan Aria agreed to give Pepe two goats.

    c. Pepe's rifle failed to fire.

14. Which event happened *last* in the plot of the story?

    a. Pepe came to the place where Juan Aria's goats had spent the night.

    b. Pepe pulled the machete out of the tiger.

    c. Pepe leaned his rifle against a tree.

15. Which one of the following facts is *most* important to the plot of the story?·
   a. the fact that a raiding tiger usually attacks more than once
   b. the fact that tigers are unbelievably swift
   c. the fact that Pepe was willing to defend himself with a machete

III. Finding Word Meanings

Now it's time to be a word detective. Listed below are five vocabulary words which appear in "The Tiger's Heart" and five *new* vocabulary words for you to learn. Study the words and their definitions. Then complete the following paragraphs by using each word only *once*.

		page
indispensable	essential; absolutely necessary	138
monotonous	dull; unvarying	139
mingled	mixed together; blended; combined	141
incredible	unbelievable	141
reality	real life	143
intense	deeply felt	
category	a particular group	
restless	unable to relax; nervous; uneasy	
survive	remain alive	
torrid	burning	

Sometimes, a movie is so boring and __16__, we become uneasy and __17__, and can hardly wait to leave the theatre. On other occasions, however, a movie may be so fascinating we watch it with deeply felt, or __18__, interest. This kind of movie can transport us away from the day-to-day __19__ of our everyday lives.

Last month, I saw a movie which fits into the second __20__. It was set in a blazing hot, or __21__, jungle in Brazil. There, a group of settlers struggled to __22__ an attack by millions of killer ants. The settlers demonstrated unbelievable, or __23__, courage. Their bravery and intelligence proved __24__ , in helping them escape from the ants. I felt admiration combined, or __25__ , with respect at the actions of this courageous group.

IV. Telling About the Case

A. Find evidence in the story which shows that Pepe was an excellent hunter.
B. Show how Pepe removed all evidence that he had killed the tiger with a machete. Explain why Pepe did this.
C. Suppose that Pepe returned to the village later. Describe the story he might have told about his battle with the tiger. It might be interesting to compare your version with those of your classmates, and to select the most popular stories.

The Town Where No One Got Off

by Ray Bradbury

Crossing the continental United States by night, by day, on the train, you flash past town after wilderness town where nobody ever gets off. Or rather, no person who doesn't belong, no person who hasn't roots in these country graveyards ever bothers to visit their lonely stations or attend their lonely views.

I spoke of this to a fellow passenger, another salesman like myself, on the Chicago-Los Angeles train as we crossed Iowa.

"True," he said. "People get off in Chicago; everyone gets off there. People get off in New York, get off in Boston, get off in L.A. People who don't live there go there to see and come back to tell."

"Wouldn't it be a fascinating change," I said, "some year to plan a really different vacation? Pick some village lost on the plains where you don't know a soul and go there?"

"You'd be bored stiff."

"I'm not bored thinking of it!" I peered out the window. "What's the next town coming up on this line?"

"Rampart Junction."

I smiled. "Sounds good. I might get off there."

"You're a liar and a fool. What you want? Adventure? Romance? Go ahead, jump off the train. Ten seconds later you'll

150

call yourself an idiot, grab a taxi, and race us to the next town."

"Maybe."

The train rounded a curve suddenly. I swayed. Far ahead I saw one church spire, a deep forest, a field of summer wheat.

"It looks like I'm getting off the train," I said.

"Sit down," he said.

"No," I said. "There's something about that town up ahead. I've got to see. I've got the time. I don't have to be in L.A., really, until next Monday. If I don't get off the train now, I'll always wonder what I missed, what I let slip by when I had the chance to see it."

"We were just talking. There's nothing there."

"You're wrong," I said. "There is."

I put my hat on my head and lifted the suitcase in my hand.

"I think you're really going to do it," said the salesman.

My heart beat quickly. My face was flushed.

The train whistled. The train rushed down the track. The town was near!

"Wish me luck," I said.

"Luck!" he cried.

I ran for the porter, yelling.

There was an ancient, flake-painted chair tilted back against the station-platform wall. In this chair, completely relaxed so he sank into his clothes, was a man of some seventy years whose timbers looked as if he'd been nailed there since the station was built.

As I stepped down, the old man's eyes flicked every door on the train and stopped, surprised, at me.

I started up the dirt road toward the town. One hundred yards away, I glanced back.

The old man, still seated there, stared at the sun, as if posing a question.

I hurried on.

It was a town where nothing happened, where occurred only the following events:

At four o'clock sharp, the Honneger Hardware door slammed as a dog came out to dust himself in the road. Four-thirty, a straw sucked emptily at the bottom of a soda glass, making a sound like a great cataract in the drugstore silence.

Five o'clock, boys and pebbles plunged in the town river. Five-fifteen, ants paraded in the slanting light under some elm trees.

All through the afternoon there was only one constant and unchanging factor: the old man in the bleached blue pants and shirt was never far away. When I sat in the drugstore, he was out front spitting tobacco that rolled itself into tumble-bugs in the dust. When I stood by the river, he was crouched downstream making a great thing of washing his hands.

Along about seven-thirty in the evening, I was walking for the seventh or eighth time through the quiet streets when I heard footsteps beside me.

I looked over, and the old man was pacing me, looking straight ahead, a piece of dried grass in his stained teeth.

"It's been a long time," he said quietly. "A long time," he said, "waitin' on that station platform."

"You?" I said.

"Me." He nodded in the tree shadows.

"Were you waiting for someone at the station?"

"Yes," he said. "You."

"Me?" The surprise must have shown in my voice. "But why . . . ? You never saw me before in your life."

"Did I say I did? I just said I was waitin'."

"You want to know anything about me?" I asked suddenly. "You the sheriff?"

"No, not the sheriff. And no, I don't want to know nothing about you." He put his hands in his pockets. The sun was set now. The air was suddenly cool. "I'm just surprised you're here at last, is all."

"Surprised?"

"Surprised," he said, "and . . . pleased."

I stopped abruptly and looked straight at him.

"How long have you been sitting on that station platform?"

"Twenty years, give or take a few."

I knew he was telling the truth; his voice was as easy and quiet as the river.

"Waiting for me?" I said.

"Or someone like you," he said.

We walked on in the growing dark.

"How you like our town?"

"Nice, quiet," I said.

"Nice, quiet." He nodded. "Like the people?"

"People look nice and quiet."

"They are," he said, "nice, quiet."

I was ready to turn back, but the old man kept talking; and in order to listen and be polite, I had to walk with him in the vaster darkness, the tides of field and meadow beyond town.

"Yes," said the old man, "the day I retired, twenty years ago, I sat down on that station platform, and there I been sittin', doin' nothin', waitin' for something to happen; I didn't know what, I didn't know, I couldn't say. But when it finally happened, I'd know it; I'd look at it and say, yes, sir, that's

what I was waitin' for. Train wreck? No. Old woman friend
come back to town after fifty years? No. No. It's hard to say.
Someone. Something. And it seems to have something to do
with you. I wish I could say—"

"Why don't you try?" I said.

"Well," he said slowly, "you know much about your own
insides?"

"You mean my stomach, or you mean psychologically?"

"That's the word. I mean your head, your brain; you know
much about *that*?"

"A little."

"You hate many people in your time?"

"Some."

"We all do. It's normal enough to hate, ain't it, and not
only hate, but while we don't talk about it, don't we sometimes want to hit people who hurt us, even *kill* them?"

"Hardly a week passes we don't get that feeling," I said,
"and put it away."

"Now," said the old man, looking at the water, "the only
kind of killin' worth doin' is the one where nobody can guess
who did it or why they did it or who they did it to, right? Well,
I got this idea maybe twenty years ago. I don't think about it
every day or every week. Sometimes months go by, but the
idea's this: only one train stops here each day, sometimes not
even that. Now, if you wanted to kill someone, you'd have to
wait, wouldn't you, for years and years, until a complete and
actual stranger came to your town, a stranger who got off the
train for no reason, a man nobody knows, and who don't know
nobody in the town. Then, and only then, I thought, sittin'
there on the station chair, you could just go up and when nobody's around, kill him and throw him in the river. He'd be
found miles downstream. Maybe he'd never be found. Nobody would ever think to come to Rampart Junction to find
him. He wasn't goin' there. He was on his way someplace else.
There, that's my whole idea. And I'd know the man the minute
he got off the train. Know him, just as clear . . ."

"Would you?" I said.

"Yes," he said. I saw the motion of his head looking at the
stars. "Well, I've talked enough." He sidled close and touched
my elbow. His hand was feverish, as if he had held it to a

stove before touching me. His other hand, his right hand, was hidden, tight and bunched, in his pocket. "I've talked enough."

The old man and I stood looking at each other in the dark. His left hand was still holding my elbow. His other hand was still hidden.

"May I say something?" I said at last.

The old man nodded.

> Now it's time for YOU to be The Reader as Detective.
>
> What can the salesman say to save his life? Read on to find out.

"About myself," I said. I had to stop. I could hardly breathe. I forced myself to go on. "It's funny. I've often thought the same way as you. Sure, just today, going cross-country, I thought, how perfect, how really perfect it could be. Business has been bad for me lately. Wife sick. Good friend died last week. War in the world. Full of boils, myself. It would do me a world of good—"

"What?" the old man said, his hand on my arm.

"To get off this train in a small town," I said, "where nobody knows me, with this gun under my arm, and find someone and kill him and bury him and go back down to the station and get on and go home and nobody the wiser and nobody ever to know who did it, ever. Perfect, I thought, a perfect crime. And I got off the train."

"How do I know you got a gun under your arm?"

"You don't know." My voice blurred. "You can't be sure."

He waited. I thought he was going to faint.

"That's how it is?" he said.

"That's how it is," I said.

He shut his eyes tight. He shut his mouth tight.

After another five seconds, very slowly, heavily, he managed to take his hand away from my own immensely heavy arm. He looked down at his right hand then, and took it empty, out of his pocket.

Slowly, with great weight, we turned away from each other and started walking blind, completely blind, in the dark.

I. The Reader as Detective

Read each question below. Then write the letter of the correct answer to each question. Remember, the symbol next to each question identifies the *kind* of reading skill that particular question helps you to develop.

 1. According to the old man, he had been waiting at the station

    a. for a few minutes.
    b. for about twenty years.
    c. all day.

 2. The salesman stated that he was carrying

    a. a briefcase   *c.* a gun.
    b. a railroad ticket

 3. Through his quick thinking, the salesman probably

    a. figured out when the next train was going to leave.
    b. sold some items to the old man.
    c. saved his life.

 4. The old man's hand "was feverish, as if he had held it to a stove." What is the meaning of the word *feverish*?

    a. hot   *b.* weak   *c.* thin

 5. Which happened last?

    a. The salesman discussed taking a vacation.
    b. Some boys plunged into the town river.
    c. The salesman stated that business had been bad and that his wife was sick.

 6. We may infer that the old man was

    a. crazy.   *b.* happy.   *c.* friendly.

7. A straw at the bottom of the glass made "a sound like a great cataract." Which one of the following expressions best defines the word *cataract*?

    a. loud shot

    b. rushing water or waterfall

    c. household pet

8. How did the salesman probably feel when the old man turned away at the end of the story?

    a. sad   *c.* relieved

    b. furious

9. Which one of the following statements expresses an opinion?

    a. Visiting strange places is always very dangerous.

    b. The old man was waiting for a stranger to appear.

    c. The salesman said that his wife was sick.

10. The story is mainly about

    a. how a salesman visits a strange town and narrowly escapes death.

    b. how an old man kills a visiting salesman.

    c. how a salesman took a trip across the United States.

II. On the Trail of Story Elements

Answer the following questions. They will help you review the following literary elements: setting, tone, style, conflict, and climax.

11. The story takes place in

    a. Los Angeles.

    b. Rampart Junction.

    c. Chicago.

12. Which expression best describes the tone of "The Town Where No One Got Off"?

    a. bright and cheerful

    b. sad and suspenseful

    c. lighthearted and amusing

13. Judging by this story, which of the following statements best describes Ray Bradbury's style of writing?

    a. He writes stories which are wildly funny.

    b. He writes stories which have a strange or mysterious quality.

    c. He writes stories based on historical events.

14. The conflict in the story is between

    a. two salesmen on a cross-country trip.

    b. a visitor to a small town and its sheriff.

    c. a salesman and an old man.

15. The turning point, or climax, of the story occurs when the salesman

    a. asked the old man how long he had been sitting at the platform.

    b. saw the old man looking straight ahead, a piece of grass in his teeth.

    c. stated that *he* had come to town to find someone to kill.

III. Finding Word Meanings

Now it's time to be a word detective. Listed below are five vocabulary words which appear in "The Town Where No One Got Off" and five *new* vocabulary words for you to learn. Study the words and their definitions. Then complete the following paragraphs by using each vocabulary word only *once*.

		page
constant	going on without stopping	152
bleached	made white by sunlight or chemicals	152
abruptly	unexpectedly; suddenly	153
psychologically	of the mind	154
sidled	moved sideways	154
foliage	leaves of a plant	
wary	careful or cautious	
solitary	alone	
unique	one of a kind; very special	
suburbs	towns or villages outside or near a city	

A few years ago, I moved from the city to the __16__ . The flowers and the beautiful __17__ are a pleasure to see. But, most of all, I enjoy these quiet hours when I can be by myself taking __18__ walks alone in the country. However, __19__ , my head (and my heart) are still in the city.

I love the city's __20__ , or never-ending, hustle and bustle. I like the unusual and __21__ places one can see there. I also enjoy the excitement and adventure it offers.

One day, I had just entered a subway station when a suspicious-looking man slowly __22__ up to me. He was wearing a faded, or __23__ , blue shirt and torn dungarees. "Hey you!" he shouted suddenly and very __24__ . I was __25__ , and cautiously waited. "Does this train go the museum?" he asked.

IV. Telling About the Case

A. The old man and the salesman each told the other a story. Summarize briefly what each character said.
B. Explain why each character indicated that he was about to commit the "perfect crime."
C. Do you think that the salesman was really carrying a gun? Explain your answer. Later, you may have an opportunity to see if most of your classmates agree with you.

"She knelt there by the fire and finished frying the slice of mushroom. If I had Pa's rifle, I'd have been willing to kill her right then. . . ."

Too Soon a Woman

by Dorothy M. Johnson

We left the home place behind, mile by slow mile. We were heading for the mountains, across the prairie where the wind blew forever.

At first there were four of us with the one-horse wagon and its skimpy load. Pa and I walked, because I was a big boy of eleven. My two sisters trotted until they got tired and had to be boosted up into the wagon.

That was no covered Conestoga, like Pa's folks came West in. It was just an old farm wagon, drawn by one weary horse, creaking and rumbling westward to the mountains, toward the little woods town where Pa thought he had an old uncle who owned a little two-bit sawmill.

Two weeks we had been moving when we picked up Mary. She had run away from somewhere that she wouldn't tell. Pa didn't want her along, but she stood up to him with no fear in her voice.

"I'd rather go with a family and look after kids," she said. "But I ain't going back. If you won't take me, I'll travel with any wagon that will."

Pa scowled at her, and wide blue eyes stared back.

"How old are you?" he demanded.

"Twenty," she said. "There's teamsters come this way sometimes. I'd rather go with you folks. But I won't go back."

160

"We're prid'near out of grub," my father told her. "We're clean out of money. I got all I can handle without taking anybody else." He turned away as if he hated the sight of her. "You'll have to walk," he said.

So she went along with us and looked after the girls, but Pa wouldn't talk to her.

On the prairie, the wind blew. But in the mountains, there was rain. When we stopped at little timber claims along the way, the homesteaders said it had rained all summer. Crops among the blackened stumps were rotted and spoiled. There was no cheer anywhere, and little hospitality. The people we talked to were past worrying. They were scared and desperate.

So was Pa. He traveled twice as far each day as the wagon. He ranged through the woods with his rifle, but he never saw any game. He had been depending on deer, but we never got any except as a grudging gift from the homesteaders.

He brought in a porcupine once, and that was fat meat and good. Mary roasted it in chunks over the fire, half crying with the smoke. Pa and I rigged up the tarp sheet for a shelter to keep the rain from putting the fire clean out.

The porcupine was long gone, except for some of the dried-out fat that Mary had saved, when we came to an old, empty cabin. Pa said we'd have to stop. The horse was wore out, couldn't pull any more up the deep-rutted roads in the mountains.

At the cabin, at least there was shelter. We had a few potatoes left and some cornmeal. There was a creek that probably had fish in it, if a person could catch them. Pa tried it for half a day before he gave up. To this day I don't care for fishing. I remember my father's sunken eyes in his gaunt, grim face.

He took Mary and me outside the cabin to talk. Rain dripped on us from branches overhead.

"I think I know where we are," he said. "I calculate to get to old John's and back in about four days. There'll be grub in the town, and they'll let me have some whether old John's still there or not."

He looked at me. "You do like she tells you," he warned. It was the first time he had admitted Mary was on earth since we picked her up two weeks before.

"You're my pardner," he said to me. "But it might be she's got more brains. You mind what she says."

He burst out with bitterness. "There ain't anything good left in the world, or people to care if you live or die. But I'll get grub in the town and come back with it."

He took a deep breath and added, "If you get too all-fired hungry, butcher the horse. It'll be better than starvin'."

He kissed the little girls good-bye and plodded off through the woods with one blanket and the rifle.

The cabin was moldy and had no floor. We kept a fire going under a hole in the roof, so it was full of blinding smoke. But we had to keep the fire so as to dry out the wood.

The third day, we lost the horse. A bear scared him. We heard the racket, and Mary and I ran out, but we couldn't see anything in the pitch-dark.

In gray daylight I went looking for him. I must have walked fifteen miles. It seemed like I had to have that horse at the cabin when Pa came home or he'd whip me. I got plumb lost two or three times and thought maybe I was going to die there alone and nobody would ever know it. But I found the way back to the clearing.

That was the fourth day, and Pa didn't come. That was the day we ate up the last of the grub.

The fifth day, Mary went looking for the horse. My sisters whimpered, huddled in a quilt by the fire, because they were scared and hungry.

I never did get dried out, always having to bring in more damp wood and going out to yell to see if Mary would hear me and not get lost. But I couldn't cry like the little girls did, because I was a big boy, eleven years old.

It was near dark when there was an answer to my yelling. Mary came into the clearing.

Mary didn't have the horse—we never saw hide nor hair of that old horse again. But she was carrying something big and white that looked like a pumpkin with no color to it.

She didn't say anything. She just looked around and saw Pa wasn't there yet, at the end of the fifth day.

"What's that thing?" my sister Elizabeth demanded.

"Mushroom," Mary answered. "I bet it hefts ten pounds."

"What are you going to do with it now?" I sneered. "Play football here?"

"Eat it—maybe," she said, putting it in a corner. Her wet hair hung over her shoulders. She huddled by the fire.

My sister Sarah began to whimper again. "I'm hungry!" she kept saying.

"Mushrooms ain't good eating," I said. "They can kill you."

"Maybe," Mary answered. "Maybe they can. I don't set up to know all about everything, like some people."

"What's that mark on your shoulder?" I asked her. "You tore your dress on the brush."

"What do you think it is?" she said, her head bowed in the smoke.

"Looks like scars," I guessed.

"'Tis scars. Now mind your own business. I want to think."

Elizabeth whimpered. "Why don't Pa come back?"

"He's coming," Mary promised. "Can't come in the dark. Your pa'll take care of you soon's he can."

She got up and rummaged around in the grub box.

"Nothing there but empty dishes," I growled. "If there was anything, we'd know it."

Mary stood up. She was holding the can with the porcupine grease.

Now it's time for YOU to be The Reader as Detective.

The children are starving, but the mushroom may be poisonous. What do you think Mary is going to do? Read on to see if you are right!

"I'm going to have something to eat," she said coolly. "You kids can't have anything yet. And I don't want any squalling, mind."

It was a cruel thing, what she did then. She sliced that big, solid mushroom and heated grease in a pan.

The smell of it brought the little girls out of their quilt.
But she told them to go back in so fierce a voice that they
obeyed. They cried to break your heart.

I didn't cry. I watched, hating her.

I endured the smell of the mushroom frying as long as I
could. Then I said, "Give me some."

"Tomorrow," Mary answered. "Tomorrow, maybe. But
not tonight." She turned to me with a sharp command: "Don't
bother me! Just leave me be."

She knelt there by the fire and finished frying the slice of
mushroom.

If I had Pa's rifle, I'd have been willing to kill her right
then and there.

164

She didn't eat right away. She looked at the brown, fried slice for a while and said, "By tomorrow morning, I guess you can tell whether you want any."

The little girls stared at her as she ate. Sarah was chewing an old leather glove.

When Mary crawled into the quilts with them, they moved away as far as they could get.

I was so scared that my stomach heaved, empty as it was.

Mary didn't stay in the quilts long. She took a drink out of the water bucket and sat down by the fire and looked through the smoke at me.

She said in a low voice, "I don't know how it will be if it's poison. Just do the best you can with the girls. Because your pa will come back, you know. . . . You better go to bed. I'm going to sit up."

And so would you sit up. If it might be your last night on earth and the pain of death might seize you at any moment, you would sit up by the smoky fire, wide-awake, remembering whatever you had to remember, savoring life.

We sat in silence after the girls had gone to sleep. Once I asked, "How long does it take?"

"I never heard," she answered. "Don't think about it."

I slept after a while, with my chin on my chest.

Mary's moving around brought me wide-awake. The black of night was fading.

"I guess it's all right," Mary said. "I'd be able to tell by now, wouldn't I?"

I answered gruffly, "I don't know."

Mary stood in the doorway for a while, looking out at the dripping world as if she found it beautiful. Then she fried slices of the mushroom while the little girls danced with anxiety.

We feasted, we three, my sisters and I, until Mary ruled, "That'll hold you," and would not cook any more. She didn't touch any of the mushroom herself.

That was a strange day in the moldy cabin. Mary laughed and told stories, and we played "Who's Got the Thimble?" with a pine cone.

In the afternoon we heard a shout. My sisters screamed and I ran ahead of them across the clearing.

The rain had stopped. My father came plunging out of the woods leading a pack horse—and well I remember the treasures of food in that pack.

He glanced at us anxiously as he tore at the ropes that bound the pack.

"Where's the other one?" he demanded.

Mary came out of the cabin then, walking sedately. As she came toward us, the sun began to shine.

My stepmother was a wonderful woman.

I. The Reader as Detective

Read each question below. Then write the letter of the correct answer to each question. Remember, the symbol next to each question identifies the *kind* of reading skill that particular question helps you to develop.

1. Pa thought that he would be back in

    a. a day or two.   *c.* about a week.

    b. about four days.

2. Mary fried the mushroom in

    a. butter.   *c.* porcupine grease.

    b. margarine.

3. The boy remembered his father's "sunken eyes in his gaunt, grim face." What is the meaning of the word *gaunt*?

    a. thin and bony

    b. round and fat

    c. smiling and cheerful

4. Which one of the following statements from the story expresses an opinion?

    a. It was just an old farm wagon, drawn by one weary horse.

    b. There ain't anything good left in the world.

    c. He kissed the little girls good-bye and plodded off through the woods.

5. We may infer that Pa

   a. scolded Mary for giving the family the mushroom to eat.
   b. got lost several times on the way back to the cabin.
   c. eventually married Mary.

6. Which happened last?

   a. The family came to an old, empty cabin.
   b. Pa came plunging out of the woods leading a pack horse.
   c. Mary found something large and white that looked like a pumpkin.

7. How old was Mary at the start of the story?

   a. 18 years old   *c.* 25 years old
   b. 20 years old

8. The boy was afraid that his father would

   a. beat him for losing the horse.
   b. complain about how dirty the cabin was.
   c. return without bringing any food.

9. Mary came out of the cabin "walking sedately." Which expression best defines the word *sedately*?

   a. angrily or furiously
   b. calmly or seriously
   c. carelessly or thoughtlessly

10. Suppose this story appeared as a newspaper article. Which of the following would make the best headline?

   a. Bear Scares Off Horse
   b. Pa Leaves to Search for Food
   c. Young Woman Risks Life for Starving Family

II. On the Trail of Story Elements

Answer the following questions. They will help you review characterization in a short story.

11. The main character in "Too Soon a Woman" is

   a. Pa.   *b.* Mary.   *c.* the boy.

12. Mary ate the mushroom, then waited to experience its possible effect. This demonstrates that Mary was
    a. very hungry.
    b. very courageous.
    c. an expert on mushrooms.

13. The scars on Mary's shoulders suggest that she
    a. was attacked earlier by a wild animal.
    b. fell on the floor of the cabin.
    c. had been beaten before she ran away.

14. In the morning, "Mary laughed and told stories, and we played 'Who's Got the Thimble' with a pine cone." This sentence shows that Mary
    a. was very childish.
    b. was happy and played all the time.
    c. acted like a mother to the children.

15. Which group of words best describes Mary?
    a. intelligent, dependable, concerned
    b. hard-working, fun-loving, unconcerned
    c. strong, smart, selfish

III. Finding Word Meanings

Now it's time to be a word detective. Listed below are five vocabulary words which appear in "Too Soon a Woman" and five *new* vocabulary words for you to learn. Study the words and their definitions. Then complete the following paragraphs by using each vocabulary word only *once*.

		page
hospitality	friendly treatment of guests	161
grudging	given without enthusiasm	161
calculate	to figure out by reasoning or by using arithmetic	161
endured	put up with; lasted	164
savoring	enjoying very much	165
consume	to use up	
obligations	responsibilities; duties	

option	freedom of choice
existence	state of being; presence
environment	the conditions which affect the growth of living things; surroundings

Imagine that you were born out West more than a hundred years ago. Try to figure out, or __16__ , what life would probably have been like? To begin with, you would not have had the choice, or __17__ , of going to the movies, or of turning on the radio or TV. No, you would not even have been aware of their __18__ . How would you have managed, or __19__ , without them?

Probably, there would have been lots of ways to use up, or __20__ , your time. For example, it is likely that you would have had more __21__ and chores than you have now. You would also proba- bly have learned to be more aware of the __22__ —the natural life around you. Possibly, too, you would have spent more time enjoy- ing, or __23__ , the friendship and __24__ of others.

Life in those days must have been very difficult. Therefore, we should not be __25__ in our admiration of our ancestors.

IV. Telling About the Case

A. Mary did not permit the children to have any of the mushroom until she had eaten some herself. Explain why Mary did this. What does this indicate about Mary?

B. How did the children feel about Mary when they saw her eating the mushroom? Why? When did the boy change his mind?

C. Why do you think the story is titled "Too Soon a Woman"?

The Wise and the Weak

by Philip Aponte

I was new in the neighborhood. I had just moved from the Lower West to the Lower East Side. Not much of a change! They were both dumps. I hated moving from the place I was brought up in, the place where all my friends lived. I had to start all over again making new friends. Days passed, and still I had no friends. Sure there were boys, but none would talk to me, and when I tried talking to them, they would just turn and walk away.

After about ten days of doing absolutely nothing, I decided to do something lest I go crazy. One evening after supper, I went downstairs and ran across a guy sitting on the stoop. I walked up to him and said, "Hello."

"Hiya," was his reply. He started walking away. I grabbed him by his arm and asked, "Why are you walking away?"

He looked at me, then at my hand on his arm. With a wise grin on his face, he said, "You'd better get your hand off, sonny. You're wrinkling the skin."

I released my grip. He looked at me sarcastically and said, "Better watch that, son, or next time I might get rough with you."

I returned his sarcasm, "Would you care to try?"

Flying fists, scratching fingernails, feet dancing on a human floor. I was getting the better of it. He went down. He got up. Down, up, down, up, like the continuous beat of a drum. I pushed him on his way, and he staggered down the street.

A smile ran across my lips. I walked down to the candy store to celebrate by buying a soda.

It was getting dark. Since I had had enough excitement for one day, I decided to go home. I walked slowly at first. Then, realizing it was rapidly getting dark, I increased my speed. I wasn't taking any chances. I opened the door to the hallway and started climbing the stairs.

"Hey, you, sonny." I turned around. It was him again, the big would-be tough guy.

"What do you want?" I asked.

"Nothing. I just wanted to meet you and make friends."

"Friends." The words seemed to scare me. Yet I had to have some friends. I walked down. He extended his hand. It missed my hand, but not my stomach. Another hand, not to mine, but to my face. This time I went down. I got up determined to teach this "big wheel" a lesson. But now, instead of one, there were six. This time I was the one who was going up and down, and I didn't like it. It wasn't long before it was over—for me, anyway. My lips were swollen, my eye was shut, my nose was bleeding. I hesitated, feeling for other injuries, fearing they had relieved me of some of my valuables. A hand came down to help me up. I was still away from it all. I got up and was about to say thanks. Yeah, it was him again, the "big tough guy." But this time I was in no mood—or rather, no condition—to fight.

"Come on, let's you and me go down to Vito's," he said.

"Vito's?"

"Yeah, the candy store."

"Oh, yeah, sure. Let's go."

We walked down and sat in one of the booths and started talking. I told him my life history, and he told me his. His name was Ron. Nice name for a not-so-nice guy. He came to the point.

"Phil, how would you like to join our club?"

"Yeah, sure," I answered. "Why not?"

"First, you'll have to prove you're an able member. You'll have to prove that you're efficient, useful."

"Efficient? Useful? I landed you, didn't I?"

"Yes, but you'll have to do much more than that. Well?"

"Yeah. Okay, what's my assignment?"

"Meet me tomorrow, here at Vito's, at, let's say about seven."

I went back home, entered through the back door, fixed my battered profile, and went to sleep. Nobody was home when I woke up the next morning. The day went slowly. I hadn't seen Ron all day. I hoped he wasn't joking. At six I went up and got my supper. At seven I was at Vito's. Ron hadn't arrived yet. I kept wondering what I was to do. I ordered a small Coke and waited for Ron. Five after seven. Then ten after, fifteen, twenty after. He'll never come, I thought.

I finished drinking the Coke and was ready to leave when the door to Vito's opened. Ron came walking in, looked around, saw me. He walked over, sat down opposite me. He was mysterious, and I was jumpy. Maybe I've made a mistake, letting him think I'm bad and bold, I thought. I've never gotten in trouble before, and I wouldn't want to. I'd better go home before something really happens.

I stood up, and then Ron spoke, "Well, Phil, ready? Ready to prove yourself?"

"Well, I, I—"

"Don't worry, Phil. It has nothing to do with defying the law." I was about to say "No," when I spotted Ron's ever-loving friends outside.

"Okay, Ron, let's be on our way," I said.

"Good boy, Phil." He laughed. I shook with fright. I had gone beyond my own reach. We walked until we got to the building across the street from where I lived. "Let's go up, Phil," he said.

"Yeah, sure," I answered. That was all I could say, "Yeah, sure." Up the stairs, first, second, third, and then the final floor. I stopped.

"Where are we going, Ron?"

"To the roof. You're not afraid, are you, Phil?" I didn't answer but just kept climbing. We walked out to the roof.

"Well, what now, Ron?"

"Wait a minute, just a minute." The building next to this was about five feet away. In between the two buildings was a four-floor drop. I walked to the ledge, looked over, and quickly jumped back. This I didn't like. The ledge was two feet high. Ron saw that I was jittery.

"No, let's just get on with the . . . the game."

Ron smiled. "Yeah, game." The door on the roof opened. Ron's friends emerged carrying a thick iron pipe a little over five feet long. They laid it from roof to roof. I turned to Ron.

"What's that for?"

> Now it's time for YOU to be The Reader as Detective.
>
> What are Ron and his friends going to do? What "game" are they going to play?
> Read on to see if you are right!

"We're going to play Tarzan." Just then more of Ron's friends appeared on our roof.

"Tarzan. What do you mean?"

"Just what I said. You know how Tarzan swings on a rope. Well, this time it isn't going to be a rope but a bar."

"Who's going to be Tarzan?"

"I'll give you one guess."

"You're crazy, Ron. That's a four-floor drop."

"Nervous, Phil? Did I say it was going to be you?"

"No, I guess you didn't, but I have to admit you had me scared there for a minute."

"You should be, Phil, because it *is* going to be you."

I stood there, stunned, even though I had suspected it from the very beginning. If only someone would call me or come upstairs to the roof, I thought to myself. It suddenly became silent. It was the first time I had really noticed how quiet a city slum can be. All of Ron's friends bowed politely, saying, "After you, Phil, after you." I took a few steps toward the iron bar, then stopped and turned, looking for a possible opening in their defense. The door to the roof was still open. My last chance, I thought. But Ron's thinking was faster than mine.

"You'll never make it, Phil. If you try and we catch you, we might—ah—accidentally on purpose throw you over." He smiled and bowed politely, saying, "After you, Phil." I walked over to the ledge.

"Look, Ron—"

"Get going, Phil!"

I grabbed the end of the bar. The other end was being held by a couple of other guys. One foot went over the side—I looked down—my hand grabbed on for dear life, and this time the expression really meant something. My other foot went over. I started on my way toward the other roof, hand over hand in agony, my feet dangling in the air. My muscles ached. My hands started sweating. A little more to go. I made it. Now to put my foot on the ledge. My foot reached the ledge. Then suddenly, without warning, one of the boys pushed it off. "Sorry," he said, "but you're not welcome on this side."

I tried again to put my foot on the ledge, but again he pushed it off. My strength, or what was left of it, was going. I pleaded with Ron to let me get over. The answer I received was a loud burst of laughter. I started back to where I had originally started. Halfway there, I felt myself slipping. I gripped tighter to the bar; I couldn't go on. Looking down, I could see nothing but darkness. I tried desperately to sit on the bar. Up I would go, then down I would slip.

I couldn't feel my hands any more. My neck muscles hurt me terribly. I tried once more, this time putting my foot on the bar, then swinging up on it. Slowly but surely I started my agonizing journey to the top. My foot was on the bar, my teeth grinding together. Up, up, up a little more. A long sigh of relief. I was sitting on the bar, drenched with sweat. It was silent again. A few seconds, minutes. A plane passed overhead, but I didn't dare look up. Why not? I didn't know, nor did I care to think about it.

"Look, Ron, what now, please? Please let me go." A few tears slid down my face. I wasn't one of them. I guess I had known it from the beginning.

"Well, Ron, well?"

"Hey, Phil, you want a glass of water or something? You want to play cards? Come on." He laughed. They all laughed. But when you're in death's grasp, you don't laugh.

"Well, Phil, we're going."

"Wait, Ron. If you go, I'll never get out of here."

"Look, Phil, if you get out of this, you're one of the boys. If you don't, well—well, you can bet we'll be at the funeral." He smiled and left, his boys following.

If I swung to one end, the other end would become unbalanced and would be likely to slide off. Another puzzle to figure out. I thought of one solution, then another, and another. No good, no good. None of them were any good. I thought of every possible angle. The only thing to do was to hope the bar wouldn't slide off the roof.

Again I hung from the center of the bar and inched up toward the ledge.

The bar started slipping. I reached for the ledge, grabbed it as the bar fell clanging below. The little pebbles of the ledge were cutting into my fingertips, but I was close. My arms extended high over my head. My body was close against the building. I lifted myself, scraping my knees and my face. Home was so near, so near. My foot reached for the ledge. One last burst of energy, and over I went, flat on my back on the roof. I lay there, my eyes closed, my lips murmuring a prayer, my legs and arms dead to the world.

I stayed there for what seemed hours. Then slowly I went back home, making sure I wasn't seen. Next day I told my mother the story. At first she didn't believe it, but after I showed her the bruises and cuts, she stood there amazed. The only thought that entered her mind was to call the police. I quickly talked her out of it, telling her it was better to have a living son than a dead one. We moved back to the West Side. Not much of a change. Both dumps, but it was a change for me—plenty.

I. The Reader as Detective

Read each question below. Then write the letter of the correct answer to each question. Remember, the symbol next to each question identifies the *kind* of reading skill that particular question helps you to develop.

1. At the beginning of the story, Phil was eager to

    a. move to the Lower East Side.

    b. find some new friends.

    c. get into trouble with the law.

2. Ron's gang forced Phil to go

    a. to the roof.

    b. to Vito's.

    c. home.

3. Which happened last?

    a. Phil reached for the ledge and grabbed it.

    b. Ron hit Phil in the stomach.

    c. Phil told his mother what had happened.

4. At the beginning of the story, Phil "ran across a guy sitting on the stoop." As used in this story, what is the meaning of the word *stoop*?

    a. bend forward

    b. small ladder

    c. porch

5. Probably, Ron was angry at Phil for

    a. beating him in a fight.

    b. stealing some money from him.

    c. trying to escape from the gang.

6. Which one of the following statements expresses an opinion?

    a. Ron forced Phil to play a very dangerous game.

    b. Phil arrived home with cuts and bruises on his body.

    c. Living in a nice neighborhood is more important than having friends.

7. We may infer that Phil and the author of the story are

    a. unusually shy.   *c.* quite strong.

    b. weak for their age.

8. How far apart were the two buildings?

    a. about two feet   *c.* about ten feet

    b. about five feet

9. The last paragraph of the story suggests that if Phil had complained to the police, the gang would have

    a. left him alone.   *c.* killed him.

    b. moved away.

10. The story is mostly about

    a. a terrifying experience in a new neighborhood.

    b. how Phil met Ron.

    c. life on the Lower East Side.

II. On the Trail of Story Elements

Answer the questions below. They will help you review the following story elements: setting, characterization, and plot.

11. What is the setting of the story?

    a. a street in a small village   *c.* the Lower East Side

    b. a fancy neighborhood

12. Which group of words best characterizes Ron?

    a. tough, mean, cruel   *c.* thoughful, helpful, gentle

    b. strong, friendly, kind

13. Phil tried to convince Ron that he was

    a. a member of a gang.

    b. bad and bold.

    c. new to the neighborhood.

14. In this story, the conflict is between

    a. Phil and his mother.   *c.* Ron and the gang.

    b. Ron and Phil.

15. Which one of the following plays the *most important* part in the plot of the story?

    a. a ledge on the roof   *c.* a movie starring Tarzan

    b. a soda in a candy store

III. Finding Word Meanings

Now it's time to be a word detective. Listed below are five vocabulary words which appear in "The Wise and the Weak" and five *new* vocabulary words for you to learn. Study the words and their definitions. Then complete the following paragraphs by using each vocabulary word only *once*.

		page
sarcastically	in a sneering manner which makes fun	170
efficient	very effective	171
jittery	nervous; uneasy	173
agony	suffering	175
drenched	soaked	175
deluge	heavy downpour	
intention	aim; plan	
changeable	something that can change	
prediction	the act of telling something in advance; a forecast	
violent	extremely rough and severe; forceful	

It was one of those __16__ days—bright one moment, cloudy the next. Just as I left school, the skies grew dark and I heard, in the distance, a loud and __17__ clap of thunder. I suddenly began to feel nervous, uneasy, and __18__. Would I be able to make it home before I got soaked in the __19__?

Usually, getting caught in the rain doesn't upset me or cause me any __20__. However, I was wearing a brand new suit, and I had no aim, or __21__, of getting it __22__ by the storm.

Unfortunately, the weather forecast that morning had not been accurate, effective, or __23__. The __24__ this morning was for a beautiful day.

"Clear and sunny today!" I shouted, __25__.

IV. Telling About the Case

A. For a moment, Phil considered running away from the boys on the roof. Why did he change his mind? Do you think he made the right decision? Why?

B. Who are "The Wise" and "The Weak" in the title of the story? Explain your answer. Would "The Test" have been a good name for this story? Offer reasons to support your answer.

"I had been away from home for 24 hours, and I was a whole new person. . . ."

Louisa, Please Come Home

by Shirley Jackson

I listened to my mother's voice over the radio. "Louisa," she said, "please come home. It's been three years since we saw you. We all miss you. We want you back again. Louisa, please come home."

Once a year I heard that, on the anniversary of the day I ran away. I also read the newspaper stories. "Louisa Tether vanished one year ago." Or two years, or three. I used to wait for June 20 as if it were my birthday.

I was living in Chandler, which was a big enough city for me to hide in. It was also near my old home, so the papers always made a big fuss about my anniversary.

I didn't decide to leave on the spur of the moment. I had been planning it for a long time. Everything had to go right. If it had gone wrong, I would have looked like an awful fool, and my sister Carol would never have let me forget that.

I planned it for the day before her wedding. The papers said they had the wedding anyway. Carol told a reporter that her sister Louisa would have wanted it that way.

"She would never have wanted to spoil my wedding," Carol said, knowing that was exactly what I'd wanted.

Anyway, everyone was hurrying around the house, getting ready for the wedding. I just walked out the door and started off.

180

There was only one bad minute, when Paul saw me. Paul has always lived next door to us, and Carol hates him more than she hates me. My mother can't stand him, either.

Of course, he didn't know I was running away. I told him what I had told my parents. I was going downtown to get away from all the confusion. He wanted to come with me, but I ran for the bus and left him standing there.

I took the bus downtown and walked to the railroad station. I bought a round-trip ticket. That would make them think I was coming back. Then they wouldn't start looking for me too quickly.

I knew they'd think I'd stay in Crain, which was the biggest city the train went to. So I stayed there only one day.

I bought a tan raincoat in a department store in Crain. I had left home wearing a new jacket. I just left it on a counter in the store. Someone probably bought it.

I was pretty sure of one thing. There must be thousands of 19-year-old girls, fair-haired, five feet four inches tall, weighing 126 pounds, and a lot of them would be wearing tan raincoats.

It's funny how no one pays any attention to you. Hundreds of people saw me that day, but no one really *saw* me.

I took a train to Chandler, where I had been heading all along. I slept on the train.

When I got to Chandler, I bought a suitcase, some stockings, and a little clock. I put everything in the suitcase. Then I was ready to get myself settled in Chandler. Nothing is hard to do unless you get upset or excited about it.

I decided who I was going to be. I was a 19-year-old girl named Lois Taylor, who had a nice family upstate. I had saved enough money to come to live in Chandler. When the summer was over, I would go to the business school there. I would need a job to pay for the school.

I stopped in a drugstore for breakfast and a paper. I read the ads for furnished rooms. It all looked so normal. Suitcase, raincoat, rooms for rent. When I asked the clerk how to get to Primrose Street, he never even looked at me.

I walked into Mrs. Peacock's house on Primrose Street. I knew this was the perfect place. My room was nice, and Mrs. Peacock and I liked each other.

She was pleased that my mother wanted me to find a clean room in a good neighborhood, and that I wanted to save money so I could send some home every week.

Within an hour, Mrs. Peacock knew all about my imaginary family. I told her my mother was a widow. My sister had just been married, and my younger brother Paul made my mother worry a lot. He didn't want to settle down.

Mrs. Peacock wanted to take care of me. She told me about a job in a neighborhood stationery store. So there I was. I had been away from home for 24 hours, and I was a whole new person. I was Lois Taylor, who lived on Primrose Street and worked at the stationery store.

Mrs. Peacock and I would read the papers during breakfast. She'd ask my opinion about the girl who disappeared over in Rockville. I'd say she must be crazy to leave a nice home like that.

Once I picked up the paper and looked at the picture. "Do you think she looks like me?" I asked Mrs. Peacock.

Mrs. Peacock said, "No. Her hair is longer, and her face is fatter."

"I think she looks like me," I said.

My picture was in the Chandler papers a lot, but no one ever looked at me twice. I went to work. I shopped in the stores. I went to the movies and the beach with Mrs. Peacock, and no one recognized me. I had done a perfect job of changing my identity.

One morning, Mrs. Peacock was reading about my disappearance. "They're saying now that she was kidnapped," she said.

"I feel kind of sorry for her," I said.

"You can't ever tell," she said. "Maybe she went willingly with the kidnapper."

On the anniversary of my running away, I treated myself to a new hat. When I got home, Mrs. Peacock was listening to the radio, and I heard my mother's voice.

"Louisa," she said, "please come home."

"That poor woman," Mrs. Peacock said. "Imagine how she must feel. She hasn't given up hope of finding her little girl alive some day."

I had decided not to go to business school, because the stationery store was branching out. I would probably be a manager soon. Mrs. Peacock and I agreed it would be foolish to give up such a good job.

By this time, I had some money in the bank, and I was getting along fine. I never had a thought about going back. It was just plain bad luck that I had to meet Paul.

I didn't stop to think when I saw him on the street. I yelled, "Paul!"

He turned around and stared at me. Then he said, "Is it possible?"

He said I had to go back. If I didn't, he'd tell them where I was. He told me there was still a reward for anyone who found me. He said I could run away again after he collected the reward.

Maybe I really wanted to go home, and that's why I yelled his name out on the street. Anyway, I decided to go with him.

I told Mrs. Peacock I was going to visit my family upstate. I thought that was funny. Paul sent a telegram to my parents.

When we got to Rockville, we took a taxi. I began to get nervous, looking out the window. I would have sworn that I hadn't thought about Rockville for three years, but I remembered it all, as if I had never been away.

The taxi turned into my street. When I saw the house, I almost cried. "Everything looks just the same," I said. "I caught the bus right there on the corner."

"If I had managed to stop you," Paul said, "you probably wouldn't have tried again."

We walked up the driveway. I wondered if they were watching from the window, and if I would have to ring the doorbell. I had never had to ring it before.

I was still wondering when Carol opened the door. "Carol!" I said. I was honestly glad to see her.

She looked at me hard. Then she stepped back, and I saw my mother and father. I was going to run to them, but I held myself back. I wasn't sure if they were angry with me or happy that I was back.

I wasn't sure of what to say, so I just stood there and said, "Mother?"

> Now it's time for YOU to be The Reader as Detective.
>
> How do you think Louisa's family will react to her return? What do you think they will do and say?
> Read on to see if you are right!

She put her hands on my shoulders and looked at my face for a long time. She was crying, and she looked old and sad. Then she turned to Paul and said, "How could you do this to me again?"

Paul was frightened. "Mrs. Tether—"

My mother asked me, "What is your name, dear?"

"Louisa Tether," I said stupidly.

"No, dear," she said very gently. "Your *real* name."

Now I felt like crying. "Louisa Tether," I said. "That's my name."

"Why don't you people leave us alone?" Carol screamed. "We've spent years trying to find my sister, and people like you just try to cheat us out of the reward money."

"Carol," my father said, "you're frightening the poor child. Young lady," he said to me, "I don't think you realized how cruel this would be to us. You look like a nice girl. Try to imagine your own mother if someone did this to her."

I tried to imagine my own mother. I looked straight at her.

My father said, "I'm sure this young man didn't tell you he's done this twice before. He's brought us girls who pretended to be our Louisa. The first time we were fooled for several days. The girl *looked* like our Louisa and *acted* like our Louisa. She even knew about family things that only Louisa—or Paul—could know. But she was not our daughter, and my wife suffers more each time her hopes are raised."

He put one arm around my mother and the other around Carol. They all stood there looking at me.

Paul started to argue with them. I realized that all I wanted was to stay here, but I couldn't. They had made up their minds that I wasn't Louisa.

"Paul," I said, "can't you see that you're only making Mr. Tether angry?"

"Correct, young lady," my father said.

"Paul," I said, "these people don't want us here." Paul was about to argue again. Instead, he turned and walked out.

I turned to follow him. My father—I mean Mr. Tether—took my hand. "My daughter was younger than you," he said gently. "But I'm sure you have a family somewhere. Go back to the people who love you."

That meant Mrs. Peacock, I guess.

"To make sure you get there," my father said, "I want you to take this." He put a $20 bill in my hand. "I hope someone will do as much for our Louisa."

"Good-bye, my dear," my mother said. "Good luck to you."

"I hope your daughter comes back some day," I told them. "Good-bye."

I gave the money to Paul. He'd gone to a lot of trouble, and I still had my job at the stationery store.

My mother still talks to me on the radio once a year. "Louisa," she says, "please come home. We miss you so much. Your mother and father love you and will never forget you. Louisa, please come home."

I. The Reader as Detective

Read each question below. Then write the letter of the correct answer to each question. Remember, the symbol next to each question identifies the *kind* of reading skill that particular question helps you to develop.

1. When did Louisa leave home?

a. the day before her sister's wedding

b. the day after her sister's wedding

c. the day of her sister's wedding

2. What did Louisa tell Mrs. Peacock?

a. She said that her mother was a widow.

b. She said that her brother didn't want to settle down.

c. Both of the above.

3. After Louisa ran away, the first thing she did was

a. buy a tan raincoat.

b. rent a room in Mrs. Peacock's house.

c. find a job.

4. Which one of the following statements from the story expresses an opinion?

a. Mrs. Peacock and I would read the papers during breakfast.

b. She'd ask my opinion about the girl who disappeared over in Rockville.

c. I'd say she must be crazy to leave a nice home like that.

5. Mrs. Peacock thought it possible that Louisa was kidnapped. Which of the following expressions best defines the word *kidnapped*?

   a. chased away
   b. carried off by force
   c. asleep for a long period of time

6. Which happened last?

   a. Carol accused Louisa of trying to cheat them.
   b. Paul sent Louisa's family a telegram.
   c. Mr. Tether gave Louisa twenty dollars.

7. Suppose that Louisa tried to prove who she was by revealing some things about her family. Probably, her mother and father would have said that

   a. she was not telling the truth.
   b. she made up the facts.
   c. Paul gave her the information.

8. Louisa bought a round-trip ticket because

   a. she knew she would need it to return home one day.
   b. she wanted to make them think she was coming back.
   c. it was cheaper than two one-way tickets.

9. According to Mr. Tether, Louisa

   a. was older than his daughter.
   b. had longer hair than his daughter.
   c. was taller than his daughter.

10. Which one of the following would make the best headline for the story?

    a. Runaway Refuses to Return to Relatives
    b. Relatives Recognize Returning Runaway
    c. Relatives Refuse to Recognize Returning Runaway

II. On the Trail of Story Elements

Sometimes, an author makes use of **irony** in a short story. Irony occurs when something takes place which is the *opposite* of what naturally would be expected. Calling a huge person "Tiny" is an example of irony. Or, it was **ironic** that the student who won the Perfect Attendance Award was absent on the day it was presented. There are many examples of irony in "Louisa, Please Come Home." Answer the following questions. They will help you review irony in a short story.

11. Each year on the radio, Louisa's mother told Louisa: "Your father and mother love you and will never forget you." This is ironic because

a. when they met Louisa, they didn't know who she was.
b. Louisa never listened to the radio.
c. the announcement was made only once a year.

12. There is irony in the fact that when Louisa

a. ran away, she got a job in a stationery store.
b. left her family, she moved to a city.
c. finally came home to stay, her parents didn't know her.

13. An ironic situation occurred when

a. Louisa left her jacket on a counter in a department store.
b. Louisa decided not to go to business school.
c. Mr. Tether told Louisa to try to imagine her own mother.

14. Louisa was being ironic when she

a. gave the money to Paul.
b. told her mother that she hoped her daughter would come back one day.
c. asked the clerk how to get to Primrose Street.

15. It was ironic that Mrs. Peacock

a. thought that Louisa didn't look at all like the girl who had run away.
b. told Louisa about the job in a stationery store.
c. wanted to take care of Louisa.

III. Finding Word Meanings

Now it's time to be a word detective. Listed below are five vocabulary words or expressions which appear in "Louisa, Please Come Home" and five *new* vocabulary words or expressions for you to learn. Study the words and their definitions. Then complete the following paragraphs by using each word only *once*.

		page
anniversary	an event which occurs every year on the same date	180
on the spur of the moment	suddenly; without previous thought	180
confusion	chaos; a bewildering condition	181
normal	usual; regular	181
identity	who and what one is; the fact of being a particular person	183
renounce	to give up completely	
variation	change	
attraction	appeal	
cherish	to hold dear; care for greatly	
discomfort	uneasiness; pain	

Have you ever had the urge to change your personality or __16__ ? It might be fun to give up, or __17__ , the way you look and act and to become a completely new individual. It does have a certain appeal, or __18__ . Every year, you would celebrate the __19__ of the *new* you.

But think of what would happen if you didn't act in your usual, or __20__ , manner. It would surely create a great deal of chaos, or, __21__ . People who know you well would be surprised at the change, or __22__ , in your behavior. It might cause them considerable suffering and pain, or __23__ .

Therefore, think twice before you act suddenly, __24__ . Remember, most people care for you and __25__ you just the way you are.

IV. Telling About the Case

A. Give reasons to explain why Louisa decided to run away.
B. Describe the steps that Louisa took to make a new life for herself.
C. Why do you think Louisa's parents acted as they did?
D. "Louisa, Please Come Home," is an extremely sad story. Do you agree or disagree with this statement? Explain your answer.

"Are you sure you want to open the chest? You do remember the message?"

Martinez' Treasure

by Manuela Williams Crosno

There was once a man named Juan Martinez who lived near the mountains. But it was so long ago no one can remember just where he lived. He had a wife named Rosa, a burro whom he called Jose, and two goats. Rosa had a small flock of chickens. Once Juan and Rosa had been young and carefree, but now they were quite old. A warm summer sun shining down many years had wrinkled their faces, so that they seemed as old as the wrinkled hills about them.

They lived where the mountains meet the desert and the forest begins. Each day Martinez walked among the trees and gathered small pieces of wood. He loaded these on Jose's back, which had become scarred and bent from many loads. At one time Jose had moved slowly because he was lazy, as are all burros. But now, with the added burden of age, he barely moved along in the midday heat.

For many years, Juan and Rosa had lived in a small house, which Juan proudly called their *casa*. From time to time they had repaired the house with adobe,* which they patted on with their bare hands. The roof leaned badly, as if it were trying, with difficulty, to shelter its owners for their few remaining years.

---

*adobe: sun-dried clay used for building

190

Juan and Rosa were very poor. In summer, they raised beans and corn to eat through the winter, and chili peppers to give the beans flavor. The red strings of peppers hanging over the roof of their *casa* in the fall were the only colorful things about it. With the small amount of money Juan received for the firewood he sold they were able to buy a bit of food. They bought flour for the tortillas and, occasionally, cheese for the enchiladas. Their few items of clothing consisted of worn-out pieces their relatives no longer would wear.

Juan and Rosa had no children. Except when they went to the village, they seldom saw a living thing—just Jose, who was not good company, their two goats, the chickens, and a few lizards that darted from their path as they went about their work.

When they were young, they had made great plans for themselves. But trying to produce food from the dry soil had been difficult. Gradually, they lost themselves in work and forgot how to laugh or play. Finally, they talked of nothing except their work and completely abandoned their early dreams. Forgetting that they had ever been happy, they accepted their monotonous and meager living as a way of life. All they knew was work and more work.

The two people were busy all day long. Martinez would be gone for hours, loading old Jose's back with wood. The next day, Martinez would go to the village, several miles away, to sell the wood. Then he would gather another load of wood, and so on, day in and day out.

For poor Rosa, each day was the same. She would rise early and milk the two goats. Then, unless it looked like rain, she would drive the goats out to eat the grass that grew sparsely on the desert. She worked hard in the fields, with the goats close by.

Sometimes she baked in the oven. It was like those built by the Indians who lived in the pueblos along the river. When Rosa made tortillas, she flattened and shaped the cakes with her hands. The cakes came out white, with some brown spots. Juan always told Rosa they were the best tortillas he had ever tasted.

One evening Juan came home much later than usual. It

had been dark for several hours. Rosa had stood at the window holding a candle, peering out anxiously into the darkness. She was looking for a sign of him. When he finally stood in the doorway, she noticed that his clothing was dusty and caked with mud. Jose stood behind him. Instead of the usual load of wood, a box or chest, about eighteen inches deep and wide, and two feet long, was tied across the burro's sagging back. Together Juan and Rosa removed the box and dragged it inside. It was very heavy and covered with hardpacked soil.

Juan told Rosa an interesting story. While Juan was gathering wood, Jose had wandered to the edge of a small arroyo, or ditch formed by rain waters from the mountains. The burro's weight caused some soil on the side of the ditch to give way. Jose slid to the bottom of the ditch. Juan walked down to get the burro. He saw the box sticking out of the side of the ditch, where the earth had crumbled. All day he dug about it with sticks, only to find it was too heavy for him to lift onto the burro's back. He dragged the chest along the top of the ditch, and then lowered it onto the burro's back and brought it home.

Rosa's first concern was for Juan. She gave him dry clothing and a bowl of hot chili. Then, they could no longer contain their excitement. They turned their attention to the box, wondering what it contained, but they could find no place where it might be opened. It had no lock, and its top could not be pried off. The chest was rusty, so they scraped it with knives. They even washed its sides in an effort to find a way to open it. They worked very late by the light of the crude candle that Rosa had carefully made. Still, they found no way to open the box, so they decided to sleep and try again in the morning.

At daybreak, they again tried to open the box. They remembered stories of hidden gold, and they were certain the chest was filled with old Spanish coins. Therefore, they did not want anyone to know of their discovery. They had to find a way to open it themselves.

But promises of riches could not keep them from their work. Soon after the first warm glow of sunlight came through their window, habit called them to their usual tasks. They hid the box away under some old blankets and baskets. All day, they thought about it and the treasure it contained.

Again they worked late into the night, trying to open the

box. They could see small letters carved into the metal-like material. But neither of them had had the opportunity to learn to read. Above the letters was a single ornament which stood out from the chest, as if for emphasis as well as design.

Juan and Rosa were strangely content now that they thought they were rich. They spent many hours trying to open the chest. While they were working, a great change came over them. They became happy, and they remained so! Now that they had gold, they did not mind that they appeared poor. They knew they could buy fine clothing! They did not mind that Jose was old. They could buy many burros with the gold in the chest! They worked without complaining, and they ate their meager food as if it, too, contained great richness.

Finally, Martinez said to his wife, "We must tell no one about the box. We must think hard how to open it. Someday I will find how to open it!"

"That is right," she agreed. "We must tell no one!"

"Even if we could open the box," added her husband, "we would be afraid to keep the gold about. We would want to store it someplace. Here it is safely hidden. We will leave it here as if we had stored it away! We are rich people!"

They put the chest away, hiding it carefully. Then they walked in lively steps around the room—almost dancing.

"Look, my Juan," said Rosa, "we are not so old!"

Now they felt as they had when they were young. So they began to do many things that were new to them. They did not work so long each day. Yet they seemed to get as much done as before. Juan sang half-remembered phrases of old songs in a shaky voice as he gathered wood. Rosa planted morning glories all around the *casa*, covering its barrenness. Their blossoms were large and blue and made the old, brown adobe look beautiful! Juan and Rosa kept the goat corral and the chicken pen clean. They even brushed Jose's tattered coat until it was almost shiny.

Happiness, it seemed, came to them in great amounts. Their relatives in the village noticed this change. There was a new freshness in Rosa's old, wrinkled cheeks. And Juan smiled so often that he seemed younger. Their eyes sparkled with gladness.

"Juan and Rosa are not so poor, after all," said their relatives. They had more respect for them, and they gave them better clothes to wear. One of Juan's brothers, Pancho, gave them a young burro to replace Jose. Pancho's wife scolded him for it later, but it brought much happiness to Juan. With the new burro, he could gather wood faster than ever and hurry back to his *casa* and the box containing his treasure. Jose was left to wander about on the desert and spend his time in idleness. Finally, he was given to Rosa's nephew's son, Cruz, a gentle lad, who was kind to him.

So the days passed and Juan and Rosa knew great joy. They had not learned yet how to open the chest, but they thought that some day they would. It seemed not to matter greatly how soon.

The years quickly came and quickly went, and finally the old people died—first Rosa, and then Juan, who died at the home of his brother, Pancho.

After Juan's funeral, Pancho's wife said to her husband, "Go and get the burro you gave to Juan. He no longer needs it, and the beast will only die."

So Pancho took his older brother Tomas with him. Together they went to Juan's house to get the burro. They found the animal standing near the corral where Juan had left him several days earlier. Before they took him with them, however, they entered Juan's house and found the chest. The two brothers tried in vain to open it.

"This," they agreed, "is why Juan and Rosa did not seem poor! The box is so heavy, it must be filled with gold!"

Together they loaded the chest onto the wagon. They hid it in Pancho's house under cover of darkness, and they told no one, except Pancho's wife, of their discovery. They reasoned that they had done more to help Juan and Rosa than their other brothers or sisters had. Therefore, they thought, the chest was rightly theirs. They knew happiness as they dreamed of what they would do with the gold. Like Juan and Rosa, they were certain that they would find the chest filled with gold pieces. Pancho's wife made plans to be the richest, the most beautiful, and the finest clothed woman in the village. She spoke of money in such hushed tones that the villagers thought her husband was going to receive an inheritance.

The brothers finally attacked the chest with heavy tools, as Juan and Rosa would never have done, but they could not split it apart! Finally, they grew impatient, and began to look for ways to get it open. Late one afternoon, Pancho stopped at the home of the village doctor, a scholarly man, who could read well.

"Doctor Gardea," he said, "my wife has been complaining of a bad headache. I wish you would come to my *casa.*" (This was not true, but Pancho's wife had agreed to pretend illness.)

It had already grown dark when Dr. Gardea came to Pancho's house. After talking with the wife, he prescribed two days of absolute quiet. He had lived in the village long enough to know that she was considered a gossip and a troublemaker. He told himself, with amusement, that this would stop her talking for a few days. The doctor was a busy man and the woman's whisperings of wealth had not yet reached his ears.

He was about to leave when Pancho asked, "Have you ever seen this old chest? It has been in my family for years!" (Pancho was never one to be concerned with the truth.) "It belonged to the father of my father, and to his father before him. It has been kept in the *casa* of Juan, my brother. Both Tomas and I have forgotten how to open it. Will you read for us what the letters say?"

The doctor stepped over to the chest and knelt beside it. Tomas and Pancho and Pancho's wife stood beside him. They were trying to hide their excitement. Their hearts pounded rapidly!

The doctor silently read the Latin words on the chest. Then he asked, "Are you sure you want to open the chest? You do remember the message?"

"Oh, yes!" replied the brothers together. "We want to open it!"

The doctor seemed reluctant. "In addition to the message," he remarked, "the letters tell just how to open it." With a quick pull, he tore aside the ornament. Then he unfastened the clasp that would allow the top to open. However, he did not lift the top, but left the house.

Pancho closed the door and locked it carefully after the doctor had gone. Now the three people could not hide their excitement! Soon they would be rich! Already they could feel the gold pieces sliding through their fingers! They quickly opened the lid.

The firelight fell on the chest, which was filled with heavy wooden statues. In their rush to get at the treasure they thought was hidden beneath the figures, they threw these on the floor. They bruised and tore their hands. Soon the box was completely empty. There was no gold in the chest.

The brothers argued with one another, and Pancho's wife became miserable. Now her neighbors would learn that Pancho was not to receive any wealth. They were to remain poor after all.

A thought came to her which she told to Pancho. "Perhaps Juan and Rosa had taken the gold and buried it under their house."

So Pancho and Tomas set about digging for the gold. They convinced themselves it had been removed from the chest and had been buried or hidden away by Juan and Rosa. They dug up all the earth around the old *casa*, never finding any treasure. They spent several unhappy years digging. They neglected their crops, and grew poorer and more miserable. Finally, the brothers quarreled and went their separate ways.

Sometime later, Pancho met Dr. Gardea in the village. Perhaps the message on the chest told where the treasure was hidden.

Pancho demanded, "Tell me what was carved into the old chest!"

> Now it's time for YOU to be The Reader as Detective.
>
> What do you think was written on the chest? Read on to see if you are right!

The doctor believed strongly in the power of the written word. He hesitated. Then he repeated the curious message to

Pancho. "Whoever owns this chest will be happy—as long as he opens it *not!*"

I. The Reader as Detective

Read each question below. Then write the letter of the correct answer to each question. Remember, the symbol next to each question identifies the *kind* of reading skill that particular question helps you to develop.

1. Juan and Rosa were certain that the chest contained
   a. wooden figures.
   b. diamonds and jewelry.
   c. gold coins.

2. When Dr. Gardea came to Pancho's house, Pancho said that
   a. he was ill.
   b. his wife had a bad headache.
   c. he had just found a wooden chest.

3. At the beginning of the story, Juan and Rosa accepted their "meager living as a way of life." What is the meaning of the word *meager*?
   a. exciting or interesting
   b. poor or lean
   c. rich or wealthy

4. Which one of the following statements expresses an opinion?
   a. We have done more to help Juan and Rosa than their other brothers or sisters, and therefore the chest is rightly ours.
   b. In summer, Juan and Rosa raised beans and corn to eat through the winter, and chili peppers to give the beans flavor.
   c. The brothers attacked the chest with heavy tools, but they could not split it apart.

5. Which happened last?

    a. Pancho and Tomas dug up all the earth around the old house.

    b. Juan dragged the heavy chest along the top of the ditch.

    c. The doctor tore aside the ornament on top of the chest.

6. Pancho gave Juan

    a. a young burro.   *c.* a new wagon.

    b. an old burro.

7. We may infer that Dr. Gardea was hesitant about opening the chest because he

    a. knew that it contained no treasure.

    b. knew that it contained wooden figures.

    c. was concerned about what the message said.

8. While Juan was gathering wood, Jose wandered to the edge of "a small arroyo." What is an *arroyo*?

    a. a ditch   *c.* a basket

    b. a village

9. In this story, what did the chest *really* represent to Rosa and Juan?

    a. hope   *c.* excellent health

    b. a life without work

10. This story is mostly about

    a. how Juan Martinez earned his living.

    b. how Pancho's wife made plans to be the richest, the most beautiful, and the finest clothed woman in the village.

    c. how an old wooden chest changed the lives of two families.

II. On the Trail of Story Elements

Another important story element is **theme**. The theme of a short story is the main idea of the story. The theme *sums up* what the story says.

Answer the questions below. Question 11 deals with theme. Questions 12–15 refer to characterization.

11. Which one of the following statements best expresses the theme of "Martinez' Treasure"?

    a. Everyone should be lucky enough to find a chest filled with gold.

    b. There is no such thing as "a pot of gold" at the end of the rainbow.

    c. As long as you have hope, it is possible to have happiness.

12. At the beginning of the story, Rosa and Juan

    a. thought only about their work.

    b. laughed and played often.

    c. were certain that their dreams would come true.

13. After Juan found the chest, he and Rosa

    a. worked harder than ever.

    b. often complained about their lives.

    c. knew great happiness.

14. Which one of the following expressions best describes Pancho's wife?

    a. cheerful and uncomplaining

    b. vain and sly

    c. quiet and shy

15. Dr. Gardea is best characterized as

    a. a gossip and a troublemaker.

    b. greedy and selfish

    c. scholarly and wise.

III. Finding Word Meanings

Now it's time to be a word detective. Listed (below) are five vocabulary words which appear in "Martinez' Treasure" and five *new* vocabulary words for you to learn. Study the words and their definitions. Then complete the following paragraphs by using each word only *once*.

		page
enchiladas	thin, flat cornmeal cakes filled with cheese or meat	191
sparsely	thinly scattered; scanty	191
emphasis	special attention	193
inheritance	something received from an ancestor	195
absolute	complete; whole	195
participate	to take part	
annual	once a year	
chefs	head cooks	
occurrence	event, happening	
insures	makes sure	

Each spring, our high school holds its __16__ International Food-Tasting Festival. It is an __17__ which everyone looks forward to eagerly.

The event has never been __18__ attended; in fact, hundreds of people always show up. This __19__ that the festival will be a complete, or __20__ , success.

Many students __21__ , or take part, in the festival. Each person prepares a favorite dish—one which has been handed down and received as part of his or her __22__ . Since the student cooks, or __23__ , come from many different backgrounds, the menu is always interesting. Special attention, or __24__ , is placed on variety. At the last festival, I tasted some __25__ for the first time. They were delicious.

IV. Telling About the Case

A. Rosa and Juan could not read the writing on the chest. What words were written there? Explain their meaning.

B. William Shakespeare once wrote: "There is nothing either good or bad, but thinking makes it so." Show how this statement applies to the story.

GLOSSARY

A

abruptly   unexpectedly; suddenly
absolute   complete; whole
absurd   foolish; ridiculous
acknowledgment   the act of admitting that something is true; agreement
acute   sharp and severe
adept   highly skilled; expert
admirably   excellently
advisable   worthy of being listened to
agony   suffering
analyzed   examined very carefully
anguish   great grief or pain
anniversary   the celebration of a date when something happened in an earlier year
annual   once a year
applicants   candidates; people who apply for something
arched   curved
asserted   stated strongly; declared firmly
assignment   a piece of work to be done
assortment   variety; collection
assurance   certainty
attraction   appeal
attractive   pleasing
avail   to make use of

B

baffled   puzzled
bankrupt   when one is unable to pay his or her debts
bizarre   very odd or unusual
bleached   made white by sunlight or chemicals

C

calculate   to figure out by reasoning or by using arithmetic
captivated   fascinated; charmed
category   a particular group
celebrity   a famous person

changeable something that can change
chefs head cooks
cherish to hold dear; care for greatly
collapse to fall down; cave in
colossal very large; enormous
commenced began; started
commotion a disturbance; violent movement and confusion
compensation something given which makes up for something else
competent able; capable
competition effort to obtain something wanted by others
complicates confuses; mixes up
comprehended understood the meaning of
confidential secret or private
confined shut in
confirmed proved to be true; established
confusion chaos; a bewildering condition
conscientiously carefully; done with great care
constant going on without stopping
consume to use up
conviction firm belief

D

deduce figure out by reasoning
dejected sad
deluge heavy downpour
depressing making sad
desirable worth having; valuable
devised planned
dignified self-respecting and proud; stately
discomfort uneasiness; pain
disqualify declare unfit or unable to do something
disregard to pay no attention to
distinguished famous or important; well known
douse to throw water on
drenched soaked

E

efficient very effective
eligible fit to be chosen
emphasis special attention
enchiladas thin, flat, cornmeal cakes filled with cheese or meat
endangered exposed to harm; put into danger
endeavor to try hard; make an effort

endured put up with; lasted
energetic very active
enthusiastically with great excitement; eagerly
environment the conditions which affect the growth of living
  things; surroundings
epidemic the rapid spread of a disease among many people in an
  area
ermine a kind of weasel or its fur
evacuate to empty
eventually finally; at the end
evidently obviously
exaggerate to make something appear greater than it is; go beyond the truth
exertion effort
existence state of being; presence

F

faculty the teachers of a school
fathom to figure out the meaning of
faulty incorrect; poorly made or done
flushed made red in color
foliage leaves of a plant
formula a rule or method for doing something
fumes vapors of smoke or gas

G

geometry a branch of mathematics which deals with circles,
  squares, cubes, triangles, etc.
glamorous fascinating; exciting
glint flash of light
grievance reason for complaint
grudging given without enthusiasm

H

hefts weighs
hoax a mischievous trick or practical joke
hospitality friendly treatment of guests

I

identical the very same
identity who and what one is; the fact of being a particular person
illuminated lighted up; made bright

image a picture in the mind
incredible unbelievable
indispensable essential; absolutely necessary
industrious hardworking
inferior lower in quality; below the average
infinite endless; vast
influential having much influence or effect on others
influenza a disease caused by a virus
ingredients parts
inheritance something received from an ancestor
injured hurt
inspiration a sudden, brilliant idea
instantaneous in an instant; very sudden; immediate
insures makes sure
intense deeply felt
intention aim; plan
intruder a person who forces himself or herself on others without
 being asked or wanted
irresistible too strong to be held back; very powerful

J

jittery nervous; uneasy
jubilant very happy; delighted

L

lecture a talk on a particular subject
liberate to set free
logic correct reasoning
lure something that attracts or appeals

M

merit value or worth
mingled mixed together; blended; combined
monotonous dull; unvarying
mystifies bewilders; puzzles

N

normal usual; regular

O

obligations responsibilities; duties
obstacles things that stand in the way or hinder

occurrence   event; happening
on the spur of the moment   suddenly; without previous thought
option   freedom of choice
ordeal   a very difficult or painful experience
overcome   to conquer

P

pampered   allowed too many privileges
participate   to take part
passion   strong liking
penetrate   to make a way through; pierce
penthouse   an apartment on the top floor or roof of a building
perceived   seen; observed
precaution   care taken in advance to prevent bad results
precisely   exactly
prediction   the act of telling something in advance; a forecast
professional   a person who works in a particular occupation for pay
profile   a side view of the face; an outline
prominent   well known or important
psychiatrist   a doctor who studies and treats problems involving the mind
psychologically   of the mind
pueblos   villages, usually of adobe and stone, built by Native Americans
pursue   to follow

R

reality   real life
rearranged   arranged in a new or different way
reciting   saying part of a lesson; answering questions in class
recognition   the act of being recognized or known
refreshing   delightful; able to refresh
rejected   turned down; not accepted
renounce   to give up completely
repulsively   in a manner which causes a strong dislike or disgust
response   answer
restless   unable to relax; nervous; uneasy
restrain   to hold back
revealed   shown; made known
rodents   rats, mice, and certain other animals which nibble or gnaw

S

sarcasm   a sneering remark for the purpose of hurting or making fun
sarcastically   in a sneering manner which makes fun
savoring   enjoying very much
scribbled   wrote quickly
sculpture   a figure carved or made out of stone, wood, clay, etc.
self-reliance   confidence in one's own ability
sidled   moved sideways
similarly   quality of being alike
sinister   evil
skyscraper   a very tall building
solitary   alone
sparsely   thinly scattered; scanty
specialty   a special or distinct line of work or profession
spectacular   sensational; highly interesting
speculate   to think carefully about; consider
squalling   loud screaming or crying
stimulated   roused or moved to action
strictly   very carefully; absolutely
suburbs   towns or villages outside or near a city
supervisor   person in charge
survive   remain alive
sustain   to endure; experience; support
symptoms   signs; signs related to a disease

T

tedious   long and tiring
temporary   lasting for a short time; not permanent
termination   ending
torrid   burning
trustees   people who are responsible for managing the affairs of a company, institution, or another person or people

U

unique   one of a kind; very special
utmost   greatest possible

V

vacancy   opening
variation   change
verified   proved to be true

vest   a short, sleeveless garment which buttons in front
violent   extremely rough and severe; forceful
virtuous   good; moral

W

wary   careful or cautious